A Radical's Search for Meaning

"Wow! What a remarkable expression of the passionate being of Dorothy Day!

With the gifted words of Monsignor Murphy, we get a real sense of the wholeness of Dorothy as woman, mother, Catholic and social justice advocate. I really felt the 'rebel' in Dorothy and how she fought for others, especially the imprisoned, the poor and for those who had no voice. Her own passion for writing and spreading the 'good news' is highlighted in Monsignor Murphy's work. This is a MUST read to get insight into the heart of Dorothy Day."

Sister Libby Fernandez, RSM
Founder and Director of Mercy Pedalers
(Formerly Director of Loaves and Fishes – Sacramento)

"Dorothy Day was a great woman. She was also a wounded woman.

The author carries us through her whole life in a clearly very impartial, inspiring way, seeing her as contemplation in action. He points out her greatness and her flaws and reminds us that it was through her flaws God called her to great holiness.

He sees her as a model for all of us. Though flawed and wounded, we are called to greatness and sainthood if we are open to God's action in our own lives. This is a very powerful and empowering book and has the potential to change people's lives for good."

Sr Stanislaus Kennedy, Founder of Focus Ireland

"Monsignor James Murphy's work, *A Radical's Search for Meaning: The Story of Dorothy Day*, challenges the reader to confront a basic quandary of faith: Can a sinner truly be a canonized saint? Murphy answers this question in the affirmative but Day's humility demurs. After a careful read, I share Msgr Murphy's well-reasoned opinion

Msgr Murphy spares little historical detail in setting forth the troubled early life of Dorothy Day, an obvious challenge to her cause for canonization. What becomes readily apparent from this work is that Day herself acknowledges her days of alcohol abuse, promiscuity, radicalization, and even an abortion, as a driving force for her ultimate spirituality and need for reconciliation with God. These experiences allowed her to better understand the desperate misery of the neediest her ministry served with ultimate grace and dignity.

Day herself was apparently not concerned with her own saintly work but focused her life on reconciliation for her sins. In Day's own words, it requires her and the reader to confront St Paul's challenge to resolve 'The Folly of the Cross'. What may be foolishness to some may be overcome by sacrifice for those who are saved by the power of God."

Hon. Robert Fracchia, retired
Superior Court of California, County of Solano

A Radical's Search for Meaning

The Story of Dorothy Day

James Murphy

ORPEN PRESS

First published 2024

Copyright © James Murphy, 2024
Paperback ISBN 978-1-78605-232-2
eBook ISBN 978-1-78605-233-9

Photographs © Department of Archival Collections, Raynor Library, Marquette University, Milwaukee, Wisconsin. Reproduced with permission.

Managed by
Orpen Press
The Spade Enterprise Centre
Hume Avenue
Park West Industrial Park
Dublin 12
Ireland

Typeset by www.typesetting.ie

Printed and bound in Ireland by SPRINTBOOKS

Dedicated to Dorothy Day,
an American saint in the making

Acknowledgments

I am grateful to the many people who supported me while writing this book, especially Marie Murray and Sister Geraldine Collins. They suggested many insightful changes to the manuscript, and Marie went further. She agreed to write the foreword, and it was through her that I connected with Eileen O'Brien of Orpen Press, who managed the publishing process with kind attention. I am also indebted to Bishop William Bishop, retired bishop of our diocese of Sacramento, who provided his usual wise advice.

And I am indebted to the hero of this book, Dorothy Day. In the course of writing, I came to admire this woman's struggle to find meaning—despite the fact that, on the one occasion I talked to her personally, she scolded me and walked away. Dorothy was in a bad mood that night. For more on that, read the Introduction.

Contents

About the Author

Monsignor James Murphy, of the diocese of Sacramento, California, holds a master's degree in journalism from the University of California, Berkeley. He has served as editor of the diocesan newspaper, the *Catholic Herald*, diocesan director of communications, pastor of three bilingual parishes, rector of the Cathedral of the Blessed Sacrament, and vicar general of the diocese. He is the author of *Saints and Sinners in the Cristero War: Stories of Martyrdom from Mexico*, and *Beauty and Horror in a Concentration Camp: The Story of Etty Hillesum*.

Foreword

If the story of Dorothy Day was a fictional work it would be dismissed as implausible. For who in a lifetime lives so many sequentially dramatic lives, inhabits such contradictory persona and embraces such ideological extremes as Dorothy Day? From hedonism to asceticism; from atheism to religion; embracing anarchic Catholicism, radical passivism and passive resistance: Dorothy Day is a woman of huge significance. She spoke truth to power, lived passionately and suffered extremely in her wild existential yearning for emotional stability, spiritual meaning and mental quiescence.

Any biographer who attempts to capture the intricacies of Dorothy Day's life and excavate the essence of the woman herself is brave indeed—yet Monsignor James Murphy does just that. In this exceptional book, *A Radical's Search for Meaning: The Story of Dorothy Day*, Monsignor Murphy confirms his reputation as an exceptional biographer, a rigorous researcher, an engaging raconteur, a compassionate investigator and a superb narrator of extraordinary lives. "Who was Dorothy Day?" he asks in his opening chapter, after which he uncovers the familial, psychological and spiritual dimensions of her life and presents her to us with elegance and empathy in his own particular authorial style.

Those familiar with Monsignor Murphy's previous publications will recognise the unique light he shines on women who are fearless in purpose and striving to reconcile their haunted spirits with the harsh realities of life. He shows how they transform the lives of others while undergoing their own startling transmutations towards eventual mystical union which sustains them in body and soul. Monsignor Murphy leaves us in no doubt that these redemptions occur through powers which exceed their own and that "the initiative is God's" in such transfigurations. God's choice of radical women for His purpose is Monsignor Murphy's thesis and as one reads the life of Dorothy Day echoes of Francis Thompson's "The Hound of Heaven" arise. So, it is no surprise to learn that Dorothy Day herself was deeply moved when she first heard a recitation of this verse. Indeed, one wonders how often was she with "heavy griefs so overplussed"? How much deep, unarticulated despair did this woman suffer in her life? How immense was her courage? How savage the ruptures of her heart? How ephemeral her happiness? How repetitive her loneliness? How did she sublimate that into the sublime but punishing work she undertook for others? This book addresses these questions.

Another facet of this book is the historic richness of the time period Dorothy Day's story traverses. We read about the San Francisco earthquake of 1906 (she was there); the sinking of the *Lusitania* and World War I; the demonstrations and hunger strikes for women's right to vote in 1917 (for which she was jailed); and the Spanish flu pandemic of 1918, during which she nursed the sick. This book transports us back to the Red Scare of 1920, the 1932 hunger march in Washington, World War II, the nuclear arms race and the Cold War. There is also the era of Cardinal Spellman, whom Dorothy picketed in 1949, and her personal defiance of the civil defense drills, for which she was jailed in 1957. We recall the Civil Rights movement, the Kennedy era of the early 1960s, the Vietnam War and the Second Vatican Council in 1965. We also learn that Dorothy Day had the distinction of the FBI holding a dossier on her with recommendations by J. Edgar Hoover that she be prosecuted for treason. What a woman! What a story!

Apart from the broad historical context of her time, Monsignor Murphy conveys Dorothy Day's tumultuous childhood and family life, her complex relationship with her father, her admiration for her mother, her thrust towards independence, and the trajectory of her lonely life. Chapter by chapter, he guides us skillfully through her college years, her bohemian lifestyle, her ill-advised relationships, the personal traumas she experienced, the choices she made, those who betrayed her, those who supported her and her pervasive hunger for purpose and meaning that drove her down so many "labyrinthine ways." Her reading preferences provide insight into the philosophical forces that shaped her compassion for the disenfranchised and the poor until we finally understand her ontological agonies as she becomes transfigured by faith.

We also meet the people whose lives influenced hers and whom she in turn influenced. We read about the establishment of the Catholic Worker movement with Peter Maurin, the newspaper *The Catholic Worker*, and the "houses of hospitality" for anyone in need of shelter or care through which she actioned her commitment to the poor but also to Christ in the "disguise" of suffering humanity. Emphasis on this spiritual dimension distinguishes Monsignor Murphy's narrative. His lens is that of a Catholic priest. His admiration for Dorothy Day is evident from his first personal encounter with her to his final words about her. His account is unapologetically imbued with his own faith in the redemptive tendency of the Holy Spirit to use human frailty to draw people to Himself. Her story is not an ordinary one. Her life is extraordinary, and she perturbs our consciences, our complacency and our belief that our attention to social injustice and human suffering is enough. We are called upon by her and by Monsignor Murphy's words to be radical in the service of others.

One might also ask what does the disposition of Dorothy Day, her writing, her life, her activism, her beliefs, her chequered history, her strength, and her frailty conjure up for Monsignor Murphy? For she evokes in him, and he in turn ignites in us, a curiosity, a yearning to understand not just this woman but humanity itself. Who are we? What is the stuff of which we are made? How do we hold within us such contradictions? How can one be saint and sinner? Who defines us in those terms and, at the end of the day, what may be said that makes our lives worthwhile?

One also wonders what Dorothy Day would protest about today: where would she pitch her tent, wave her banner or be jailed for? Would she protest at this planet under threat, at authoritarian regimes, democracy undermined, despotic populism, or would she march against wars waged around civilians? Would she challenge public platforms on which vitriol has free reign? Perhaps she would confront counterfactual advocacy, demagoguery or as a journalist fight stridently against disinformation, misinformation and inequalities of power. Or would she weep at homelessness, displacement, refugees fleeing the tyranny of one regime to arrive at the antagonism of another? *A Radical's Search for Meaning: The Story of Dorothy Day* asks us to ask ourselves where we stand on these issues. What have I done with my life? What plight moves me? What do I challenge in the world today?

This is a book for everyone. It is a riveting story about an amazing woman written by an exceptional author with erudition, impartiality and finesse. Inspired by Monsignor Murphy's unwavering faith that those who search for meaning find it, I have no doubt but that this book will find its way to all who need to read it.

Dr Marie Murray, Clinical psychologist
Adjunct professor, School of Psychology,
University College Dublin

Introduction

When Dorothy Day spoke at the Newman Center in Sacramento, California, in 1971, I was there as a reporter. As associate editor of our diocesan newspaper, I was the one assigned to cover this noted speaker's visit to our area. My memory of that night, however, was not the story of her conversion to Catholicism—I knew that already—but a response she gave to a question from a student about the effectiveness of her work. Feeding all those poor people was fine and dandy, this student said, but what was she doing to address the roots of poverty? "Nothing," Dorothy answered. "Well, what's the point of it all then?" the student asked. Dorothy's answer was five words: "The folly of the Cross!"

The student was surprised by her abrupt answer, and so was I. And I got another surprise a few minutes later when I asked her to give me an interview for our newspaper. She refused. "Why do you need an interview?" she said. "Didn't you hear my talk?" Then she looked me up and down and asked, "Are you a priest?" When I answered yes, I got a scolding for doing a job that rightly belonged to lay people. Dorothy Day was in a bad mood that night.

Truth be told, I wasn't offended by her blunt dismissal. If anything, I was awed in the presence of this venerable activist, by then in her seventies with white hair that was braided and wound around her head like a crown. I had heard about Jesuit Father Dan Berrigan who burned draft cards to protest the Vietnam War and did time in prison for it, but here was a woman who had been doing that kind of thing for forty years, long before Berrigan was born. She was a prophetic voice, a sign of contradiction, a famous Catholic convert who cast a long shadow across the American religious scene.

Two years later, I saw her again (as a reporter), this time in Southern California, where she joined labor leader Cesar Chavez in picketing vineyards whose owners refused to allow workers to unionize. It was a hot summer day, and she was one of the oldest people walking the picket line. By then arthritis had restricted her mobility, and she had to take frequent rests, sitting on the chair-cane she brought with her. Not surprisingly, onlookers gathered around her at such moments, eager to meet the famous activist with the big straw hat. Even the sheriff's deputies chatted with her, while she for her part chided them for wearing guns on their belts. As biographer Jim Forest commented, it was "like a grandmother patiently admonishing children about war toys".[1] The following day, she and Chavez were arrested along with a large number of supporters, including thirty nuns and two priests, and they were taken to a nearby minimum-security facility where they spent the following days saying the Rosary. "Our barracks were alive with prayer," she wrote at the time.[2] After twelve days, the charges were dropped and the prisoners were released. It was the eighth time Dorothy had been arrested.

I have been studying the life of Dorothy Day ever since: her personality, her brilliant mind, her interest in Marxism, her conversion to "the folly of the Cross". (In using the phrase "the folly of the Cross", Dorothy was referring to the scandal of Calvary, the triumph of failure described in the New Testament whereby Christ saved the world through weakness rather than strength. More broadly, the phrase expresses the inverse logic that characterizes the way God does things, a logic that contradicts the wisdom of human beings. As Saint Paul said, "the wisdom of this world is folly in the eyes of God."[3])

What my study made me realize was that this was not a typical radical activist who loved to join controversial causes and organize soup kitchens. Yes, she was all of that, but there was more to her than that. I learned that her activism was the outward fruit of an inner torment, a life-long search for meaning that culminated in a life of great holiness. After her conversion, she spent a couple of hours a day in prayer, but it is easy to overlook that side of her life. Many people do. As Mark and Louise Zwick say in their book *The Catholic Worker Movement: Intellectual and Spiritual Origins,* "It is a mystery that this important aspect of her life and spirituality can be almost erased by its simple omission or by the stroke of a pen, when she herself declared so many times how important it was to her."[4] Dorothy's lifelong friend Sister Peter Claver put it this way: "They [commentators] won't give God the credit."[5]

Dorothy Day was a saint in the estimation of many. But she was also a flawed person who lived an early life of promiscuity that nearly destroyed her. It was the grace of God that saved her and set her "ablaze" with the fire of heaven, to use the words of biographer William D. Miller. "If anyone has looked from the darkness of despair to heaven's light it was she," Miller has written. "And if anyone has struggled, day after day, to tell of the beauty of that light to all who would listen, it was she."[6]

That is what makes this story so inspiring. It has all the drama of a Saint Augustine and, like Saint Augustine's story, it says something important about sainthood. It reminds us that saints are flawed people just like the rest of us—some very flawed—but those flaws are not an obstacle to holiness and sainthood. Quite the contrary. It is precisely through those flaws that God brings us to holiness if we are open to His action in our lives. Dorothy Day was someone who was indeed open to that divine action, as we will see in the following chapters.

1.

Who Was Dorothy Day?

A Brief Overview of Her Life

On November 9, 1997, an important Mass was celebrated in Saint Patrick's Cathedral, New York, to mark the hundredth anniversary of the birth of Dorothy Day. The celebrant that day was Cardinal John O'Connor, the high-profile head of the New York archdiocese who was also arguably the most knowledgeable American churchman in the U.S. military. Before becoming a bishop, O'Connor had spent twenty-seven years as a chaplain in the U.S. Navy and enjoyed the respect and admiration of the military establishment. By the time he retired from military service, he was the Chief of Navy Chaplains with the rank of rear admiral.

The person he was honoring that day, however, could hardly be described as a lover of the U.S. military. Dorothy Day was a famous anti-war radical who offended many a conservative American with her books and newspaper columns. She had opposed U.S. entry into the First World War and the Second World War, and police arrested her several times for protesting the annual civil defense drills during the Cold War. She marched on picket lines to protest the nuclear arms race and the Vietnam War and expressed horror at clergymen sprinkling holy water on U.S. bombers, and giving them names like "Holy Innocents" and "Our Lady of Mercy".[7] Even those in the top echelons of the federal government took notice. The FBI had a 500-page file on her, and FBI Director J. Edgar Hoover recommended three times to the U.S. Attorney General that she be prosecuted for treason.

It must have been a surprise for those not in the loop, then, to see the Archbishop of New York honor this woman with a special Mass, not to mention hearing what he had to say in his sermon that day. He called Dorothy Day "a truly remarkable woman" who had combined a deep faith and love for the Church with a passionate commitment to serving the poor and saving lives.[8] It was precisely because she was such a committed person of faith, he said, that she became such a radical Christian. The more he read about her, he said, "the more saintly a woman she seems to be".[9] The real purpose of the Mass at Saint Patrick's, it turned out, was not to celebrate the anniversary of her birth, but to float an idea. O'Connor was considering proposing her for canonization.

By this time, it should be noted, attitudes about war and peace had changed in New York. Gone was the era of Cardinal Francis Spellman, the churchman who had famously supported American foreign policy around the world without a hint of self-doubt. (He was Dorothy Day's bishop for a significant part of her life.) Cardinal O'Connor, despite his military background, turned out to be very different. As archbishop, he became an outspoken critic of war and militarization, and he condemned U.S. intervention in many trouble spots around the world, including Central America, Afghanistan and Yugoslavia. He also questioned the policy of spending vast sums of money on nuclear weapons systems that only made the world more dangerous. Ironically, it was his experience as a chaplain on the Vietnam battlefields that forged those outspoken convictions. "No priest can watch the blood pouring from the wounds of the dying, be they American or Vietnamese of the North or South, without anguish and a sense of desperate frustration and futility," he had written back then. "The clergy back home, the academicians in their universities, the protesters on their marches are not the only ones who cry out, 'Why?'"[10] Chaplain O'Connor's views on war and peace were closer to those of Dorothy Day than many imagined at the time.

Now, as archbishop, he was floating the idea of canonizing her, and he invited interested people to write to him. He also organized a lengthy meeting with those who knew her best, and the feedback he eventually got from those sources convinced him that he should indeed follow through with his idea. He would be failing in his duty if he didn't act, he said, adding: "I don't want to have on my conscience that I didn't do something that God wanted done."[11]

That was over twenty-five years ago. Since then, the canonization process for Dorothy Day has been steadily moving ahead. Cardinal O'Connor's successor, Cardinal Edward Egan, formally established the Dorothy Day Guild in 2005 to promote the cause, and his successor, Cardinal Timothy Dolan, in 2012 proposed Dorothy Day's cause to the annual meeting of the American bishops, who gave the idea overwhelming support. In 2021, Cardinal Dolan officially closed the local phase of the investigation process (again during a Mass in Saint Patrick's Cathedral) by putting a wax seal on the last of the archival boxes containing 50,000 pages of evidence on Dorothy's holiness. The boxes were then shipped to Rome. Following Vatican rules, those boxes had to include transcripts of everything Dorothy had written—which was considerable—along with interviews with those who knew her well. About two hundred people had worked on the project, half of them volunteers. Her cause is now in the hands of the Vatican Congregation for the Causes of Saints.

Predictably, the controversy that followed Dorothy Day throughout her life has also been following her through this canonization process. "Was Dorothy Day Too Left-Wing to Be a Catholic Saint?" the *New York Times* asked. In his homily at the cathedral, the newspaper said, the cardinal skimmed over Dorothy's political beliefs about war and peace and focused on her far from sinless life. "He reduced her to 'she lived a life of sexual promiscuity and she dabbled in communism,'" one of Dorothy's granddaughters said. "What worse enemy could we have, saying those things about her."[12] There is a point to that criticism, but it is exaggerated. Dorothy Day was indeed a political radical and that should not be downplayed, but neither should the Saint Augustine-like story of her conversion that culminated in a life of mysticism. Both aspects are part of her remarkable story. One homily can't cover everything, but the 50,000 pages of evidence in the archival boxes certainly did.

Controversy comes with the territory when canonizing saints. The canonization of Junípero Serra by Pope Francis in 2015 was met with bitter condemnation from some Native Americans who believe he was part of a colonial system that caused the extinction of their people. History has plenty of other examples. Saint Thomas Aquinas was among several thirteenth-century theologians who were condemned by the then archbishop in Paris. He is now considered the greatest of the Scholastic philosophers, and his comprehensive synthesis of Christian theology and Aristotelian philosophy has had a major influence on Catholic doctrine for centuries. Saint Augustine is another example. He was famous for his early life of sin, which he wrote about at length in his *Confessions.* "God, grant me chastity and continence, but not yet," he famously said.

Growing up in a family of five children

Dorothy Day was born in New York City, not far from the Brooklyn Bridge and the waterfront; the towers of the bridge were probably visible from her house. She was the third of five children, the first three of whom came in ten-month intervals: Donald in 1895, Sam Houston in 1896, and Dorothy in 1897. Her sister Della was born in 1899, and baby John in 1912. "I can remember well the happy hours on the beach with my brothers," she wrote, "fishing in the creeks for eel, running away with a younger cousin to an abandoned shack in a waste of swamp."[13]

Dorothy's father, John Day, was a sports writer whose specialty was the race track. He carried a Bible around with him, and his columns about racing were often laced with biblical and Shakespearean allusions—this despite the fact that he professed to be an atheist. His friends considered him an eccentric. "He was gruff, surly, smart, respected," according to one nephew. "Just about everybody referred to him as 'Judge Day'."[14] A tall, well-dressed southerner who loved the "American Way", he disliked Jews, African Americans, radicals, and foreigners. He didn't have much time for Catholics either. "Nobody but Irish washerwomen and policemen are Catholic," Dorothy remembered him saying.[15] But he loved the outdoors and the horses. He was fonder of horses than he was of children. He ate with his children on Sundays only, and that meal was conducted in gloomy silence. They could hear each other swallow, Dorothy remembered.

Judge Day believed that women had no place in barber shops or news rooms, so it should be no surprise that he disapproved of how his elder daughter turned out. He referred to her as "the nut in the family", and Dorothy responded with silence.[16] She says little about him in her autobiographies, and throughout her life she tended to avoid contact with him. "We children did not know him very well, so stood in awe of him", she wrote, "only learning to talk to him after we had left home."[17] It didn't help matters that Dorothy's personality was very like that of her father. They were "two peas in a pod in some ways and each as bullheaded as the other," her granddaughter Kate Hennessy said.[18]

Dorothy's relationship with her mother was very different. Grace Day was a frequent presence in Dorothy's writing, both in her autobiographies and in her journals and newspaper columns. Dorothy characterized her mother as a delightful personality and resourceful housewife. Grace never let difficult economic times discourage her, and she was never afraid of hard work. After a long day washing clothes and bed sheets, she used to dress up for dinner and regale the children with stories of her youth and the exploits of her ancestors. (Her father, Napoleon Bonaparte Satterlee, was wounded in the U.S. Civil War.) Dorothy deeply admired her mother and stayed close to her all her life. Even in her wild twenties, when she was drinking heavily and getting into reckless affairs, she continued to communicate with her mother.

Growing up in the Day family meant being constantly on the move. Dorothy was just beginning school when John Day got a job in California covering the racetrack scene for a San Francisco newspaper, and the family immediately boarded a train going west. While waiting for the furniture to make its way around the tip of South America, the family rented a furnished house in Berkeley and then settled in an attractive bungalow in Oakland, near the racetrack. It was a happy time for the sports writer. In his mid-thirties, he was doing the kind of work he loved, studying horseflesh and drinking with the men who gambled their savings on it. But on April 18, 1906 everything changed.

At 5:12 a.m. the earth began to shake and wouldn't stop for what seemed like an eternity. By the time it was over, eighty percent of San Francisco City was in ruins (including the plant that printed John Day's newspaper), and over three thousand people died from the collapsing buildings and the fires. Dorothy remembers her brass bed rolling back and forth and chandeliers crashing to the floor, but the house remained standing. There was less damage on the Oakland side of the Bay, which was why many of those who fled San Francisco took the ferry to

Oakland. The racetrack that John Day was covering became a camping ground for earthquake victims.

What eight-year-old Dorothy remembered most vividly was the human warmth and willingness of people to help each other. "Mother and all our neighbors were busy from morning to night cooking hot meals," she wrote later. "They gave away every extra garment they possessed. They stripped themselves to the bone in giving, forgetful of the morrow. While the crisis lasted, people loved each other."[19] The example of community that Dorothy saw at that time left a deep impression on her, and she mentioned the experience many times throughout her life.

But community spirit notwithstanding, Dorothy's father knew they would have to move again. Within days, the family boarded the train for Chicago without their furniture (they sold it for cash in Oakland) and without prospects of a job. In Chicago, they rented what they could afford, a dingy tenement apartment over a tavern in a poor part of town that had neither trees nor a blade of grass. It was the family's first experience of humiliating poverty, and even young Dorothy felt embarrassed. Not wanting to be seen by her friends entering the door of an ugly tenement building, she often passed by her own door and instead entered a more impressive building on nearby Ellis Avenue.

But the ever-pragmatic Grace made the best of it. She got her hands on leftover fabrics, made them into curtains, and used fishing rods to hang them. She turned orange crates into bookcases and nail kegs into kitchen stools. She had no sewing machine, but that did not stop her. She handstitched the family's shirts and dresses. Dorothy never forgot the strength her mother displayed during those days. "All our clothes were beautifully made and laundered no matter how poor we were," she said.[20]

And no matter how spartan the food was, Grace continued to dress up for the evening meal as if they were in one of Chicago's most expensive restaurants.

With no job in sight, John Day decided to write a book—it would be a best-selling adventure novel, he assured his wife. With an ashtray on one side and a glass of whiskey on the other, he pounded the typewriter for weeks that ran into months, while the children were on strict orders not to disturb their father's concentration. The novel never got published, but Papa Day did eventually find a job as the sports editor of a Chicago newspaper, and the Days were able to move to a better part of town. They eventually settled in a large residence near Lincoln Park that gave the family a sense of security against the icy wind and "steady whirl of snowflakes" that beat against the windows all winter. Dorothy had many happy memories of that home as family members enjoyed each other's company, and a smell of fresh bread filled the house. She makes special mention of the library—yes, it had a library—with an attractive fireplace where they "burned huge lumps of soft coal that hissed and sputtered and sent out blue and rose flames".[21] The family gathered there every night to read around a large round table, and they often made cocoa over the fire before going to bed. But John Day's silent presence reigned. "There were no picture books, detective stories or what father termed 'trash' around the house," Dorothy wrote. "We had Scott, Hugo, Dickens, Stevenson, Cooper and Poe. I can remember sneaking romances into the house, lent me by my friends in school, but I saw to it that they did not reach my father's eyes."[22]

A Passion for Reading and Writing

The breadth and depth of Dorothy Day's reading was astonishing. Those were simpler days, of course, with no distraction from television and social media, but even allowing for that the extent of her reading was unusual even from an early age. "I can remember books I read, children's stories, and the fascinating *Arabian Nights* which I read when I was six," she wrote.[23] In high school, she loved English composition, and she was so good at Latin and Greek that she translated Virgil's *Georgics* and *Bucolics* just for fun; they were not on her course. By the age of fifteen, she was reading socialist authors, in particular Upton Sinclair's book *The Jungle* about poverty in America. She called Sinclair the Dickens of the American scene. "The very fact that *The Jungle* was about Chicago where I lived, whose streets I walked, made me feel that from then on my life was to be linked to theirs, their interests were to be mine; I had received a call, a vocation, a direction to my life," she said.[24]

This passion for reading only grew when she went to the University of Illinois at Urbana (on a scholarship that she won because of her proficiency in Latin and Greek). When she found many of the classes at Urbana boring, she began to skip them, which gave her even more time with her beloved books. Reading was now consuming her life. She worked extra hours—washing and ironing clothes and watching children—just to buy more books. "A friend of mine once told me she had to close her eyes when she walked past a bar," she said. "I told her I knew how she felt. I have to close my eyes when I walk by a bookstore and even a library."[25]

But what she read was not "trash", to use her father's term. Dorothy Day loved the nineteenth-century novelists, and she read them as if her life depended on them: Charles Dickens' *David Copperfield, Great Expectations,* and *Little Dorrit;* Leo Tolstoy's *War and Peace, Anna Karenina,* and *Resurrection;* Fyodor Dostoevsky's *The Brothers Karamazov, Crime and Punishment,* and *The Idiot.* She said she read every Dostoevsky novel she could get her hands on, and his tortured search for God touched her deeply, as did Tolstoy. "I was moved to the depths of my being by the reading of these books during my early twenties when I, too, was tasting the bitterness and the dregs of life and shuddered at its harshness and cruelty," she said.[26] Throughout her life she kept going back to those books, quoting passages from them to make a point about God or man. "This would have been a far lonelier life," she said, "if I hadn't 'met' Mr. Dickens and Mr. Tolstoy, and some others."[27]

She also had a passion for writing, something that blossomed at the University of Illinois. On campus she joined the Scribblers Club, a student group that controlled the campus newspaper, and that paper soon began to publish her articles. She also had some articles published in the town newspaper, some of them criticizing the working conditions of the students at the university, which "got me into hot water", she wrote.[28] These pieces were the initial steps in a journalism career that would span the rest of Dorothy Day's life.

The classes on campus continued to be a bore, and a change in the family fortunes caused Dorothy to rethink her plans about college. When John Day's Chicago newspaper closed and he got a job with the New York *Morning Telegraph* in spring 1916, Dorothy decided she had had enough of Urbana. She moved back to New York with the family. But living under the same roof as her father was more difficult than ever. Everything about Dorothy irritated her father: her chain-smoking (even though he was a chain-smoker himself), her liberal views on everything from capitalism to pre-marital sex, her desire to become a journalist despite her gender. As biographer William D. Miller says, it was hard enough for John Day to hold on to the few certitudes he had—his wife, the beauty of horseflesh in motion, his old-fashioned morality and sense of family order—without having to put up with a daughter he considered a communist.[29] Dorothy vowed to get out of the house and support herself as soon as she could, but it wasn't easy. Armed with her folder of newspaper clippings from Urbana, she began to look for a job as a reporter, but most New York dailies wouldn't let her get past the reception desk. The city editors who did talk to her sounded just like her father; they told her urban reporting was not for girls.

After five months of disappointments, she got an interview with the managing editor of a socialist daily, *The Call,* who was sympathetic, but told her flatly that he didn't have the money to pay her. She didn't expect much money, she said, and besides they really should have a female reporter in the newsroom. Five dollars a week would be fine, she said, which was no more than what many factory workers earned. Apparently, he was impressed by her spunk. He took her on for a month at five dollars a week and then kept her on at twelve dollars a week. Working from noon to midnight, Dorothy threw herself into her new job, writing articles about the kinds of issues that socialist newspapers covered: strikes, evictions in the slum tenements, food riots, anti-war meetings, fires and other incidents that caused loss of life. Among the people she interviewed was Leon Trotsky, one of the architects of the Russian Revolution, and Margaret Sanger, the birth-control advocate. But after only seven months, she quit that job over a dispute with the editor and got a job with another publication, *The Masses,* a journal that prided itself on taking pot shots at capitalist bourgeois morality. The writers there were considered the intellectual aristocracy of the American Left.

Forces outside her control determined that her time at *The Masses* would not last long either. The U.S. Post Office suddenly withdrew the magazine's mailing permit, and the editors were indicted on charges of sedition. Dorothy ended up putting out the final edition of the publication on her own. In effect, she was the managing editor at the age of nineteen, and among the things she learned was how to dummy up a paper for the printers. That was a skill that would be useful years later when she started her own newspaper. She eventually worked for another radical publication called the *Liberator,* a magazine that some called the American voice of the Russian Revolution. By that time, Dorothy's experience in the craft of journalism was getting deeper, as was her reputation as a communist sympathizer.

Civil Disobedience

It was at this time that Dorothy Day saw the inside of a jail for the first time, and it happened without much forethought. A friend of hers, Peggy Baird, had just done a stint in jail in Washington, D.C., for demonstrating in front of the White House for women's right to vote, and she planned to go back to D.C. for an even bigger protest. Would Dorothy join her? The answer was yes. Dorothy supported the right of women to vote, she said, and anyway she was between jobs. Why not go! The next day, November 10, 1917, Dorothy and Peggy were among some forty women who showed up at Lafayette Park, across the street from the White House, with banners and colored ribbons of purple and gold across the bodices of their dresses. "There was a religious flavor about the silent proceedings," Dorothy wrote. "To get to the White House gates one had to walk halfway around the park. There were some cheers from women and indignation from men who wanted to know if the President [Woodrow Wilson] did not have enough to bother him, and in wartime too!"[30]

As expected, the protesters were arrested, but they did not end up in jail; the judge postponed sentencing and let them go. But when the feminists went back to the White House and repeated their protest, they were arrested again, and this time they got thirty days. The leader got six months. The suffragists immediately announced that they were going on hunger strike until they received better treatment from the jail authorities. They wanted the same privileges as political prisoners in Europe, they said: the right to wear their own clothes, receive mail without censorship, and have access to their own doctors and lawyers. It worked. By the tenth painful day of fasting, to their surprise, their demands were met, and the suffragists called off the hunger strike.[i] Dorothy gladly ate the plate of chicken

---

[i]   On the eighth day of the fast, Peggy Baird decided to accept food, and that decision momentarily broke Dorothy's resolve. When Peggy slipped a crust of bread soaked in milk into Dorothy's cell, Dorothy ate it, but then felt guilty and resumed the fast.

that was provided and read a bundle of letters that had arrived from her New York friends.[31] A week later, the suffragists got an even bigger surprise. "A pardon signed by the President," the warden told them. "Now you'll be home to eat Thanksgiving dinners."

"We don't want a pardon," one of the women responded; "we have committed no crime to be pardoned for."

"All the same, out you go," the amused warden said.[32]

Dorothy Day did not share the jubilation of the other suffragists that day, however. This was her first experience of jail, and the suffering she saw among the regular jail population shocked her so much that she lost all interest in the White House protesters and their cause. "A heartbreaking conviction of the ugliness, the futility of life came over me so that I could not weep but only lie there in blank misery," she wrote. The fact that she and her fellow protesters would be free after thirty days meant nothing to her when she knew that "behind bars all over the world there were women and men, young girls and boys, suffering constraint, punishment, isolation and hardship for crimes of which all of us were guilty."[33] Dorothy was haunted by the bitterness and despair she had tasted in the novels of Dostoevsky and Tolstoy, but this was not a book. This was real. She continued to shudder at the harshness and cruelty of it all, and now she asked the kinds of fundamental questions the suffragists did not ask: Is there not more to human existence than this? What is the meaning of life? What is the meaning of death? Why is there so much injustice in the world?

Dorothy Day eventually converted to Catholicism, to the shock and bewilderment of her radical friends, and she founded the Catholic Worker movement, a network of houses of hospitality that offer food, shelter, and other services to the poor. Today there are some 150 of those houses across the U.S. and about twenty-five more in other countries. But her political radicalism didn't stop. She never voted, and never accepted government money for her charity work. She also refused to pay federal income tax; she called it a war tax. In taking that stand, she assumed she was safe from the law because all staff (including Dorothy) lived together in community and received no personal income that could be taxed. That assumption proved to be wrong. In April 1972, she received a bill for $296,359 from the Internal Revenue Service, which included unpaid taxes plus fines and interest. Dorothy was caught off-guard and began to worry about how this ominous move would end. Would the federal government confiscate the Catholic Worker building in Manhattan and whatever other property the movement owned?

One easy solution to this would have been to apply for tax-exempt status as a charitable organization, but Dorothy refused to do that. "We are told by Jesus Christ to practice the works of mercy, not the works of war," she said. "And we do not see why it is necessary to ask the government for permission to practice the works of mercy, which are the opposite of the works of war."[34] In the end, it was the spotlight shone by the press that saved her. Newspaper editors (and religious leaders) immediately came to her defense, and an editorial in the *New York Times* wondered if the IRS did not have better things to do than shut down the charitable works of a lady who was doing so much good.[35] Faced with the glare of negative publicity, the IRS dropped the case, and Dorothy continued to boycott the tax collectors.

Her civil disobedience on the streets also continued. She was arrested eight times for supporting various controversial causes: refusing to participate in civil defense drills in the fifties; protesting U.S. involvement in the Vietnam War in the sixties; supporting California farmworkers on strike in the seventies. And as her profile grew, so did her speaking schedule. "There are meetings every morning, afternoon and evening," she wrote about one visit to the U.S. West Coast. "This morning I speak at the Good Shepherd House at nine, then catch the ten thirty bus and go out to Pullman where Washington State College is, get there at twelve thirty to speak again. Tomorrow four meetings."[36] So went her busy life, travelling by bus around the country, speaking in churches, seminaries, university clubs, trade union halls, from New York to Vancouver, down the coast to San Diego, across the South to New Orleans, down to Tampa and West Palm Beach, and up though Atlanta to New York.[37] She stayed in Catholic Worker houses a lot of the time, but also in convents and monasteries. There were three things she always carried in her bag: her diary, her breviary, and a jar of instant coffee, and she refused to say which was the most essential.

She also appeared regularly on television and radio talk shows, becoming a voice of conscience on war, peace, and the poor. One of the nation's pre-eminent magazines, *The New Yorker*, did a two-part profile of her. But while some wanted to canonize her, others demonized her. She was labeled a "northern communist whore" in the American South when newspapers in Memphis and Tennessee attacked her for supporting unions for the (Black) sharecroppers. Inside the Catholic Church, she also faced criticism from many who found her political views too extreme. When she refused to take the side of General Franco in the Spanish Civil War, the steady stream of visits by priests and seminarians dried up. They wrote off the movement as "a band of nuts, Catholic puritans, or marginal radicals". The circulation of the *Catholic Worker* fell by 100,000. As granddaughter Kate Hennessy commented, "Dorothy found herself relegated to the fringes of the Catholic Church, much like a poor and batty aunt who can't be gotten rid of and is embarrassing in what she could come out with at indelicate moments."[38]

But those critics were more than outweighed by the high-profile leaders who continued to admire her. When she was in Rome for the final session of the Second Vatican Council, Cardinal Leo Suenens invited her to an afternoon discussion in honor of Frank Duff (the founder of the Legion of Mary), and everyone clapped when she introduced herself as the founder of the Catholic Worker movement. Back in the U.S., the list of people who came to visit her in lower Manhattan was like a Who's Who of Catholicism: French philosopher Jacques Maritain, English writer Evelyn Waugh, the saintly Mother Teresa of Calcutta. Cardinal Bernard Cook of New York arrived at her door one day with birthday greetings from Pope Paul VI. Meanwhile, the Jesuit magazine *America* did a special issue about her life and work, and Notre Dame University gave her its highest honor, the Laetare Medal. Her picture appeared in *Life* and *Newsweek* along with positive profiles, and *Time* magazine included her in a cover story about "Living Saints". Those honors continue to this day. In 2022, the New York City authorities named one of the newly built ferries between Manhattan and Staten Island after her.

Dorothy never let this attention go to her head, however. She looked at her rising fame with a detached eye because, as one writer noted, she had learned from the Gospels that the most important events occur in the margins of history, in obscure and unexpected places, not on the front pages of newspapers. "Too much praise makes you feel you must be doing something terribly wrong," she once said.[39] In the last decade or two of her life, she turned down at least fifteen invitations from Catholic colleges to be awarded an honorary degree, citing as a reason her disgust at the subversion of education by the U.S. military.[40]

Dorothy Day wrote seven books, three of which are auto-biographical. *From Union Square to Rome* (1938) is an apologia addressed to her communist friends who could not understand why she joined a regressive organization like the Roman Catholic Church. In it, Dorothy takes pains to explain the teaching of the Church to radicals. (In 2024 a new edition of this book was released by Orbis Books with a foreword by Pope Francis. In 2023 an Italian translation of it was released by the Vatican, also with a foreword from Pope Francis.) *The Long Loneliness* (1952) is Dorothy's best-known autobiography, in which she gives a more comprehensive account of her spiritual struggles, her conversion to Catholicism, and the founding of the Catholic Worker movement with Peter Maurin. I will draw heavily from both of these autobiographies in the course of telling this story.

Dorothy's novel, *The Eleventh Virgin* (1924), describing the sexual struggles of a woman in her early twenties, is a thinly veiled autobiography and cannot be ignored. The racy details in that novel embarrassed her later in life when she became a Catholic celebrity, and she wished she could visit every library in the country and destroy every copy. But it turned out to be a lucrative book. Pathé purchased the movie rights and paid her $2,500—a lot of money in those days. (A dollar in 1924 would be worth more than eighteen dollars today.) She used that money to buy a cottage on the beach on Staten Island. More on that later. They never did make a movie out of the book, for which Dorothy was probably thankful.

I am also indebted to four biographers, contemporaries of Dorothy Day who knew her well: Robert Coles, author of *Dorothy Day: A Radical Devotion*; Jim Forest, author of *All Is Grace: A Biography of Dorothy Day*; William D. Miller, author of *Dorothy Day: A Biography*; and Dorothy Day's granddaughter, Kate Hennessy, author of *Dorothy Day: The World Will Be Saved by Beauty: An Intimate Portrait of My Grandmother.* The two volumes of Dorothy Day's writing published twenty-five years after her death, *The Duty of Delight: The Diaries of Dorothy Day,* and *All the Way to Heaven: The Selected Letters of Dorothy Day*, are also invaluable sources of information. I am thinking in particular of her letters to her common law husband, Forster Batterham, that are included in the second volume. Along with *The Eleventh Virgin,* those letters use the kind of erotic language that is not found in the rest of her writing and thus are a window into her private life. If Dorothy Day is canonized, as I hope she will be, we will have somebody in the Calendar of the Saints whose romantic life is known in intimate detail, more than any other saint I can think of.

But that is not the most significant thing to note about Dorothy Day. A clue to the most significant side of her life can be found in the title she gave her 1952 autobiography, *The Long Loneliness.* What did she mean by that title? "I meant a spiritual hunger", she told Robert Coles, "a loneliness that was in me, no matter how happy I was and how fulfilled in my personal life." In another conversation with Coles, she put it this way: "As far back as I can remember I asked questions about 'life'—why we're here and where we're going."[41] One day, at a young age, she asked her father why people become what they become and do what they do. After thinking about it, her father told her it was a matter of temperament. Dorothy was not satisfied with the answer. She was looking for something deeper.

Understanding that spiritual hunger, that search for meaning, is the key to understanding Dorothy Day's life. It began in her childhood, and it lay behind pretty much everything she did and everything she wrote in her adult life.

2.

College Years

The Girl Who Cursed God

"All my life I have been haunted by God," Dorothy Day wrote in the first chapter of her autobiography *The Long Loneliness.* She borrowed those words from a character in *The Possessed,* Fyodor Dostoevsky's masterful novel about the need for faith in God and the futility of nihilism.[42] It was from novels like *The Possessed* that Dorothy got much of her religious sense when she was a young adult.

But how much religious instruction did she get as a child? The answer is none from her parents. Her mother was Episcopalian, but didn't go to church or practice any form of prayer. And her father professed to be an atheist. But when the rector of their local Episcopal church in Chicago called on the family one day, he convinced Grace to allow the children to attend church if they wanted—which they did. The two older boys joined the choir for a short time, and Dorothy continued to attend the church after her brothers left. She was baptized and confirmed in that church, and it was there that she developed the sensitivity to the beauty of God's creation that made her want "to cry out for joy".

"The song thrilled in my heart, and though I was only ten years old, through the Psalms and canticles I called on all creation to join with me in blessing the Lord," she wrote. Her idea of heaven became one of fields and meadows, sweet with flowers and songs, in which even the laughing gulls and the waves on the shore would play their part: "If only I could sing, I thought, I would shout before the Lord, and call upon the world to shout with me."[43] But at the same time, she was saddened by the fleeting nature of joy and wondered what that meant. Why do experiences of happiness suddenly evaporate, or turn into sorrow so quickly, she wondered.

It was also at this early age that she had what she called her "first impulse towards Catholicism". Her family was living in a poor neighborhood in Chicago at the time, and one morning she went upstairs to play with the Barrett children, who lived in an apartment above the Days'. Finding nobody in the kitchen, she looked around and found herself in the front bedroom, where Mrs. Barrett was on her knees saying her prayers. The children had all gone to the store, Mrs. Barrett said, and went on with her prayers. Something joyful touched Dorothy Day's soul that morning. "I felt a warm burst of love toward Mrs. Barrett that I have never forgotten," she wrote, "a feeling of gratitude and happiness that still warms my heart when I remember her. She had God, and there was beauty and joy in her life."[44] Years later, when Dorothy dabbled in Marxist ideology, there were still "moments when in the midst of misery and class strife, life was shot through with glory. Mrs. Barrett in her sordid little tenement flat finished her breakfast dishes at ten o'clock in the morning and got down on her knees and prayed to God."[45]

Rebelling Against Sunday Worship

By the time Dorothy went to college, however, her views had changed dramatically. At the University of Illinois at Urbana, she turned against all churches because religion was a purely Sunday affair that had nothing to do with the rest of the week, she said. She didn't want to be associated with churchgoers anymore. "Both Dostoevsky and Tolstoy made me cling to a faith in God, and yet I could not endure feeling an alien in it," she wrote. "I felt that my faith had nothing in common with that of the Christians around me … and the ugliness of life in a world which professed itself to be Christian appalled me."[46] Then one day in class (one of the few classes she attended), the professor made a comment about religion that got her attention. Religion had brought great comfort to people throughout the ages, he said, and we should not condemn it, but those who are strong do not need it; religion is a crutch for the weak. At least that is what Dorothy picked up from him. "I felt then for the first time that religion was something that I must ruthlessly cut out of my life," she wrote. "As a matter of fact, I started to swear, quite consciously began to blaspheme in order to shock them [churchgoers]. I shocked myself as I did it … but I felt that it was a strong gesture that I was making to push religion from me."[47]

Dorothy was rebelling against more than religion at this time. She also avoided socializing with the students on campus because all they talked about was football, sororities, and the movies. Listening to their idle chatter was as boring as sitting in the classroom. To make matters worse, she refused to use the student housing, but instead took an inexpensive room off campus that turned out to be a horrible place. It was bare and uninviting, no carpets, no heating, and she had to pile her books on the floor. It was so cold at night that she found it difficult to study, and even in bed it was hard to keep warm. "The winds from the prairies howled into the shabby old house, and the heavy snows and sleet beat against the window," she wrote.[48] In the evenings she could study in the university library, but when she returned to her room she went to bed immediately, and in the morning she was so cold and hungry she did not want to get up. She felt abandoned and desperately missed the warmth of home. "I was so completely homesick that I could neither eat nor sleep and I paced the brick-paved walks of that small college town with tears streaming down my face, my heart so heavy that it hung like a weight in my breast."[49]

Meanwhile, she kept herself busy reading the kinds of radical books she had begun reading during her last year in high school: American writer Jack London; Italian novelist Ignazio Silone; Russian playwright Anton Chekhov; Russian revolutionaries Peter Kropotkin (whom she looked upon as saint), Vera Figner, and writer Maxim Gorky. She also read the history of the U.S. labor movement, and her heroes were those who campaigned tirelessly for the eight-hour workday and the five-day week. At that time, only eight percent of American workers were unionized, and ten-hour workdays were common. Dorothy could see the results of this all around her: disabled men with no insurance who had to depend on public charity when they could no longer work; exhausted workers whose strength had been drained from them by the industrial system in which they were trapped; farmers gaunt and harried by debt; mothers weighed down with children at their skirts, in their arms, in their wombs. "All this long procession of desperate people called to me," she wrote.[50] A slogan she picked up from the Marxists became her motto: "Workers of the world, unite! You have nothing to lose but your chains." That battle cry made more sense to her than some verses from the Book of Psalms. Like a Dostoevsky character, she cursed God and decided that religion was an insidious crutch, the opiate of the people.[51]

The Tragic Life of Rayna Prohme

In her autobiography *From Union Square to Rome*, Dorothy says that her two years at the University of Illinois would have been a waste of time were it not for one thing: the friendship she formed with Rayna Prohme. That friendship made it all worthwhile, she says, and her descriptions of the relationship are striking. They are among her most heartfelt pieces of writing.

Her first encounter with Rayna was from a distance. Rayna was the one person she remembered seeing on the train from Chicago, full of students on their way back to the university. "She stood out like a flame with her red hair, brown eyes and vivid face," Dorothy said. "She had a clear, happy look, the look of an honest and sincere person."[52] Their first conversation, some months later, began as a business meeting. Dorothy had applied for membership of the Scribblers Club and submitted the required two samples of her writing, one of which was about her experience of going for three days without food (except salted peanuts) because she was spending too much money on books. Rayna and another Scribblers member met her over coffee to compliment her on her writing and to let her know that she had been accepted as a member of the club. Dorothy and Rayna immediately connected; each saw qualities in the other that she admired.

Dorothy found herself talking to someone like herself, someone with radical views who loved books and had little time for the "foibles of the fraternity-sorority crowd and their adoration of Coach Zuppke".[53] Rayna, for her part, appreciated Dorothy's intelligence and determined spirit, and she was especially struck by her article on having to go hungry for three days. What came from this meeting was a friendship that was destined to leave an indelible mark on Dorothy Day's memory and character. As William D. Miller has said, the University of Illinois should have a plaque somewhere on the campus that tells the story of these two remarkable women and their passion for justice, one destined to be a famous Catholic and the other a famous communist.[54]

Part of this friendship was Rayna's gentle determination that Dorothy would not go without food again. Because she came from a wealthy Jewish family and had more money than the average student, Rayna was able to take on Dorothy as a kind of pet project, insisting that the two girls share everything, even her expensive clothes. Eventually she invited Dorothy to come and live with her, for free, in a Jewish boarding house off campus, while at the same time making sure that Dorothy did not feel beholden to her in any way. For Dorothy the timing could not be better. "I had not had enough food or sleep for a long time and I had become morbid," she wrote.[55] She found a new joy in life as she and Rayna went to concerts together and attended lectures on socialism and feminism. They also loved to talk about the books they were reading, while enjoying picnics on the prairie "under the limitless sky while the smell of sweet clover filled the air and the meadow larks pierced the quiet with their songs".[56] When summer came, Dorothy spent some time with Rayna's family on their farm outside Chicago, and Rayna in turn visited Dorothy's family in New York.

"Whatever she did she did with her whole heart," Dorothy said about Rayna. "If she read, she read. If she was with you, all her attention was for you. She was single-minded, one of the pure of heart, and her interest in life was as intense as her interest in books." She was "a character one meets but once in a lifetime".[57] As William D. Miller put it, "What Raya had was a mystical sense of the oneness of all. She had a vision of community, and it was this that lighted her soul and gave her that special radiance that Christians ascribe to saints."[58]

Ten years later (the two girls had gone their separate ways by then), one of those who became enchanted by Rayna's radiant personality was the journalist and novelist Vincent Sheean, who was visiting China in 1927 to interview the leaders of the Chinese communist revolution. While he was in Hankow (now Wuhan), a *New York Times* reporter told him to interview a red-haired American girl by the name of Rayna Prohme who had become a revolutionary leader there. Mad as a hatter, a complete Bolshevik, but a nice girl, the *Times* reporter said.[59] Sheean did indeed talk to Rayna and was immediately taken with her sincerity and purity of intention. He met her again in Moscow a few months later when he went there to cover the tenth anniversary of the Bolshevik Revolution. (Rayna and the other communists had been forced to flee Hankow when the city fell to Chiang Kai-shek in 1927.)

Rayna met him at the train station when he arrived in Moscow and immediately took him to Red Square to see the parade marking the tenth anniversary of the Russian Revolution, which had been going on all day. The two spent hours watching that grandiose spectacle as Joseph Stalin stood triumphantly in a high box near Lenin's tomb, saluting communist delegations from all parts of Europe and Asiatic Russia as they marched by in the enormous square below.

By now, Sheean had fallen in love with Rayna and was trying to get her to give up her obsession with Marxism and come back to the U.S. with him. But Rayna said no. She was planning to officially join the Russian Communist Party, she said, and she was ready to begin courses at the Lenin Institute, where she would be trained in techniques for promoting world revolution. The best Sheean could do was talk her into going out with him one more time—to have "a bourgeois evening" during which they would "dance the night away", he said.[60] But that final outing did not work out as Sheean had hoped. After having dinner at Moscow's Grand Hotel, Rayna said she wanted to attend another communist celebration that was going on that evening. Sheean reluctantly agreed to go with her, but it was obvious they were not on the same page.

The ceremony was held in a historic marble palace, thronged with communist delegates from all over the world, with huge banners everywhere proclaiming (in several languages) the words "Workers of the world unite" in letters of gold on red. Rayna and her companion ended up in one of the galleries overlooking the ballroom, and what she saw below filled her with emotion. "As the roars of the crowd came up to us," Sheean wrote later, "crashing in successive, irregular waves like thunder, she looked at me and I could see her eyes were brilliant with tears."[61] Sheean had had enough. He left before the end of the ceremony and spent the rest of the evening alone, drinking himself into a stupor.

The following day, Rayna suddenly fainted and lost consciousness. It turned out that she was suffering from encephalitis, an inflammation of the brain that killed her a few days later. Her funeral had all the trappings of a state event, an occasion of triumphalism for the communist hierarchy, but an experience of unspeakable sadness for anyone who knew Rayna personally. Sheean, who was present, described it all in his book *Personal History*, published in 1935: the bier draped in the Red flag and covered with golden flowers; the hours-long walk in the bitter cold across Moscow to the crematorium, while a band played the revolutionary march; the delegations of Chinese, Russian and American communists, many of whom had never met Rayna; the presence of Madame Sun Yat-sen, the revolutionary leader with whom Rayna worked in Hankow (who walked in the procession even though she was not dressed for the freezing temperatures); finally, the arrival at the crematorium, where the bier was placed on the platform, and the signal was given to flip the switch. "And the golden mass of Rayna, her hair and her bright flowers and Red flag sank slowly before us into the furnace."[62]

Meanwhile, Dorothy Day (who had lost contact with Rayna) knew nothing of these exploits in China and Russia until she read Vincent Sheean's book. Shocked at the news of Rayna's death, she was overtaken by a heart-rending sadness, a sadness that stayed with her for the rest of her life. She devotes significant space to this tragic story in both autobiographies, *From Union Square to Rome* and *The Long Loneliness,* and she reread Sheean's account many times throughout her life. According to Miller, she was still rereading it shortly before she died.

What haunted Dorothy was not only that her friend was cut down "at the peak of her glowing, radiant life", but also that she never found an answer to life's most fundamental questions.[63] In their student days, both girls had been passionate seekers of truth, and both believed they had found an answer in the world revolution being promoted by the Marxists. But Dorothy eventually became disillusioned when she saw what was happening in Russia under Stalin, and she came to realize that there must be a deeper meaning to human existence than this brutality. Rayna never reached that conclusion. Would she have come around had she lived long enough? Dorothy believed the answer was yes. Her sincere love of truth, Dorothy believed, would have eventually brought her to her senses and "would have forced her to give up the Communist Party."[64]

"And now her dust, in an urn, reposes in Moscow", Dorothy wrote with a broken heart, "and I alone pray for her soul, for I am the only one she knew who has a faith in the resurrection of the body and life everlasting."[65] [ii]

When Dorothy wrote those words, she was already a Catholic with the faith and teaching of the Catholic Church to support her. But she continued to be haunted by Rayna's tragic end and kept asking herself the question: Where is Rayna now? Is she in Heaven? To answer that question, she eventually turned

---

[ii]   She is quoting from the Creed that is said every Sunday at Mass.

to the writings of Jacques Maritain and François Mauriac,[iii] who said that people who dedicate their lives to improve the lot of others—even communists like Rayna—have "a title to salvation" and therefore belong to "the invisible unity of the Church".[66] Dorothy had concluded that Rayna Prohme was a Catholic despite herself, an anonymous member of the Church.

But we are getting ahead of ourselves. A lot will happen in Dorothy's life before she gets to that blessed stage.

[iii] Jacques Maritain (1882–1973) was a French philosopher and convert to Catholicism. He was influential in the development and drafting of the Universal Declaration of Human Rights, and wrote more than sixty books. François Mauriac (1885–1970), a French novelist, poet, and lifelong Catholic, was awarded the Nobel Prize in Literature in 1952.

3.

Greenwich Village Friends

Everybody Was Writing a Book

On March 21, 1917, thousands of people gathered in New York's Madison Square Garden to celebrate a historic revolution that had just taken place in Russia. Faced with massive strikes and an army that ignored his orders, Czar Nicholas II had been forced to abdicate, bringing an end to an ancient dictatorship that had seemed destined to go on for ever. Dorothy Day was one of those who came to celebrate that day. "I felt an exultation, the joyous sense of victory of the masses as they sang 'Ei Euchnjem,' the workers hymn of Russia," she wrote. That hymn was a "mystic gripping melody of struggle, a cry for world peace and human brotherhood."[67]

Arise, ye prisoners of starvation!
Arise, ye wretched of the earth!
For justice thunders condemnation,
A better world's in birth.

Dorothy's friend and co-worker at *The Call* newspaper, Mike Gold, was with her that day. His views about the wretched of the earth and world revolution were as radical as hers. When the newspaper was put to bed at midnight, he and Dorothy often took long walks along the streets of Manhattan, or sat on the piers overlooking the East River, and talked into the early morning hours about President Woodrow Wilson's entry into the First World War and the military draft (which Mike avoided by fleeing to Mexico the following year). They read Tolstoy together and decided that the only religion they would tolerate would be Tolstoyan religion—a "Christianity that dispensed with churches or a priesthood".[68] Sometimes Mike sang Yiddish folk songs he had learned growing up. Eventually he fell in love with Dorothy, and the two got engaged despite the disapproval of Mike's Orthodox Jewish mother. When he introduced Dorothy to his mother, she didn't speak to her, but simply offered her food; after Dorothy left she broke the dish she had eaten from. Dorothy and Mike eventually broke off the engagement because Dorothy was not ready for marriage. Mike's feelings were hurt, but he soon got over it, and the two continued to be friends. If nothing else, their common interest in literature and communist revolution kept them together.

It was Mike who introduced Dorothy to the Provincetown Playhouse, the old brownstone building in the Greenwich Village section of Manhattan whose downstairs rooms had been converted into a small theater. His interest there was a play he had written that was about to be rehearsed by the Province-town Players, while Dorothy's interest was in getting to know the playwrights who hung out there. And Dorothy had another incentive. The theater was warm, and the places she was renting at the time were not. "It was a bitterly cold winter and the rooms I lived in were never really heated," she wrote. "There was a coal shortage that winter and heatless Mondays were instituted."[69] Moreover, there was a stench in one of the places she rented that seeped in through the cracks, and at night cats prowled the building, shrieking "with almost human voices as though that stairway was haunted by lost souls".[70] Dorothy stayed away from her digs as much as she could, and her reward was the many friends she made in the Greenwich Village literary circle, all of whom were older than she was.

Mike Gold eventually became a successful novelist and literary critic—his 1930 semi-autobiographical novel *Jews Without Money* was a bestseller—but he continued to be a die-hard communist revolutionary, and he continued to hate all organized religion. Meanwhile, Dorothy Day eventually became a dedicated Catholic and lifelong pacifist. But the two remained close friends despite those differences, and when Mike died in 1967 she wrote a heart-warming obituary about him in the *Catholic Worker* newspaper. "His faith in the class struggle and violent revolution never wavered over the years," she wrote, but nonetheless "I considered him my oldest friend."[71]

Peggy Baird was another lifelong friend Dorothy met in Greenwich Village. She was the girl who talked Dorothy into getting arrested outside the White House in November 1917. Peggy was a free spirit who smoked and drank heavily, was very attractive to men, and had no inhibitions. She was not an intellectual. She liked to draw sketches and for that reason considered herself a credible member of the Greenwich Village literary set. But the room she rented was a mess. When Dorothy dropped in one morning to visit her, she was still in bed, hair uncombed, smoking a cigarette, and sketching nude women on a pad propped up against her knees, while several other incomplete drawings were scattered over the floor. She was delighted to see Dorothy, and immediately instructed her to fix a cup of coffee for each of them. Dorothy would find the gas burner and everything else she needed behind the curtain that divided the room, she said.

Then Peggy said, "Just strip off your clothes—the room's warm enough—and while you're drinking your coffee, I'll sketch you."[72] It was not what Dorothy was expecting. Taking off her clothes was not the kind of thing she would normally do, not even if her mother or sister asked her, but that day she surprised herself by doing it. Within seconds, she was curled up on the sofa without a stitch of clothes on, comfortably smoking a cigarette. Had men begun to make love to her yet, Peggy asked, adding that Dorothy was "just the type". Yes they had, Dorothy said, but she found it immature and adolescent, not done "violently enough to be convincing". It was purposeless, as though they did it because everyone else was doing it, she said. "I don't get half so many thrills as I thought I would when I became grown up and untrammeled," she said. Peggy suggested that "unawakened" would be a better word than "untrammeled."[73]

Dorothy was not the uninhibited type, but neither was she a prude. She enjoyed Peggy's company and admired her openness and adventurous spirit. In some ways, her own views about sexual freedom were similar to Peggy's. What right did a man have to ask that his wife present herself to him as a virgin on their wedding night, she asked her mother once.[74] But Peggy was probably right when she said Dorothy's sexuality was unawakened. Dorothy was going through a dormant phase at this time. She was "more sexless and unemotional" at the age of eighteen than she had been at fifteen, she said in her semi-autobiographical novel *The Eleventh Virgin*.[75]

Many years later, Peggy volunteered at the Catholic Worker movement and ended up becoming a Catholic. When she fell victim to a slow cancer, people gathered around her just as they had done years earlier when she was living in that messy room in Greenwich Village. "It is wonderful how young people and old turn to Peggy, who is always calm, equable, unjudging," Dorothy said as her friend was dying.[76]

Eugene O'Neill

When Dorothy Day walked into a room, people noticed her. At twenty years old, she was "tall and thin, more bones than flesh, with a strong, clear jaw and large oddly slanting blue eyes," her granddaughter wrote, "thin and straight brown hair with auburn highlights, and hands and feet that are long, narrow, and graceful".[77] She was also sociable, very literate, and expressed herself like a well-educated person. But there was another side to this young lady. If somebody provoked her, or treated her unfairly, she would not take it lying down. When she was arrested for picketing at the White House, for example, she bit the hand of a guard who was treating her with no respect, and "had the satisfaction of seeing him start back and swear viciously". Then two other guards held her hands above her head to avoid being bitten, but she got her revenge on them by kicking them in the shins.[78] [iv]

On another occasion, while riding in a taxi in New York, the driver assaulted her in a Jewish cemetery in Yonkers, but she was having none of it. She fought back like a Shakespearean shrew, biting him until he bled and then demanding that he drive her to the train station. Incredibly, he obeyed her, and when he began to curse she shut him up by lecturing him about the way he was living his life.[79] Apparently, he was more scared of her than she was of him. Dorothy also knew how to drink. It was said that she was the girl "the gangsters admired" at the saloon because "she could drink them under the table".[80] As Kate Hennessy wrote, she was a "self-possessed girl of twenty, cool-mannered, tweed-wearing, drinking rye whiskey with no discernible effect and smoking like a chimney at a time when women weren't allowed to smoke in public".[81]

Agnes Boulton, a pulp fiction writer, remembered seeing Dorothy enter the Golden Swan saloon in Greenwich Village one night, followed by two down-and-out men she had picked up on the icy steps of a nearby church. "I saw at once that this girl was a personality, an unusual one," Boulton said. "It was odd because she looked and dressed like a well-bred young college girl." She was extremely attractive in a strange kind

---

[iv]   Dorothy later told friends that the suffragists filed a suit against the U.S. Government claiming that she had been permanently injured by that incident. According to Dorothy, however, what she suffered was nothing more than a bruise on her back. She did not say how the suit ended, or if she ever got financial compensation.

of way, Boulton said, and gave the impression of being a sort of "genius".[82] In other words, she was not the kind of refined young lady one would expect to see in a shabby saloon like the Golden Swan. Here is Boulton's recollection of that night:

"Hello, Christine. Where's Gene O'Neill?" Dorothy asked as soon as she walked into the back room. "Well … you ought to know," Christine said, laughing. (Christine ran the food service in the Provincetown Playhouse.) Looking through the swinging doors that separated the back room from the bar, Dorothy saw O'Neill standing at the bar. "Oh, there you are, Gene O'Neill" she shouted.[83] She then ordered three rye whiskeys, one for herself and one each for the two men she had brought with her. She and the two men then sat down at Christine's table, and Dorothy stretched out her long legs, closed her eyes, and began to sing. The song she sang was the popular American ballad "Frankie and Johnny", based on the true story of a 22-year-old African-American girl who shot her boyfriend when she caught him sleeping with another girl.

Dorothy must have been the youngest person in the back room that night (Mike Gold was three years older, Peggy Baird seven, and her friend O'Neill nine), but she was the center of attention and enjoyed every minute of it. She ordered another drink for the two men, one of whom then stumbled over her long legs as he went to the toilet. By this time, her friend O'Neill had come from the bar area to the back room to hear young Dorothy's performance.

The Golden Swan saloon was not an attractive establishment. "It was a dark, dirty, and dank place," says Kate Hennessy, "the sawdust covering the floor smelled of urine, and two pigs lived in the cellar."[84] But it was the regular meeting place for the

Greenwich Village bohemians, partly because it was convenient (just around the corner from the Provincetown Playhouse) and partly because it was inexpensive. The owner was an Irishman and former prize fighter by the name of Tom Wallace who lived upstairs and used to bang the floor with his cane when he wanted something. His customers included pickpockets, pimps, and members of the Hudson Duster gang, but those rough types usually drank in the bar area where women were not allowed. The Provincetown Players met in the back room, which they nicknamed the "Hell Hole", a more apt image for the place than the gilded swan that hung over the main entrance. But the Hell Hole had more ideas and ideals than any bar in the Waldorf-Astoria Hotel, Peggy Baird used to say.

More ideas and ideals, but not much money. Those who frequented the Hell Hole were mostly aspiring writers who had little more than the clothes on their backs and a typewriter. Like Dorothy, they were barely able to pay five or six dollars a month for a furnished room without heat, let alone find a more upscale saloon to socialize in. But socialize they did, often till the early hours of the morning. "No one ever wanted to go to bed, no one ever wanted to be alone," Dorothy said.[85] Their ideas were often contradictory—their thinking was narrow and parochial and yet they considered themselves citizens of the world—but they felt free to say and think what they wanted. "Atheism, anarchism, socialism, vegetarianism, women's rights, free love, free speech, free thought—it was all in the air," says Hennessy.[86] Everyone dreamed of writing a book, or a play, and some of them did eventually become famous writers.

Dorothy's friend Gene O'Neill was one of those who became famous. Better known as Eugene O'Neill, he had already become the most prominent playwright in the Provincetown Playhouse, and he would eventually become eminent on a much bigger stage, despite his personal problems, or perhaps because of them. His father, Irish immigrant actor James O'Neill, was an alcoholic, and his elder brother, Jamie, drank himself to death at the age of forty-five. Eugene was also an alcoholic and suffered from a tremor in his hands (possibly a form of Parkinson's disease) that got worse as he got older. During the last ten years of his life, he could not write. By then he had become one of America's greatest playwrights, having won the Pulitzer Prize for Drama four times and the Nobel Prize in Literature in 1936. His plays are known for their themes of tragedy and death, themes Dorothy had already been pondering through her reading of Russian literature.

That winter of 1917, O'Neill and Dorothy spent many nights together, drinking in the Hell Hole and walking the streets of Manhattan in the bitter cold. They got on well together, despite the age gap, for a number of reasons. One was their similar histories. Both were native New Yorkers, both were reporters who had dropped out of college, and both liked to write about the poor and outcasts of the earth. Another reason was her intelligence and her appreciation of his plays. He trusted her opinion and even gave her manuscripts to read. But a more important reason, as William D. Miller points out, was O'Neill's vulnerable personality, which appealed to Dorothy's compassionate side. "He was, as a personality, a maladjusted egocentric, a type to which she was drawn as some people are drawn to stray dogs," Miller says. "He exhibited all the signs of the wounded and suffering soul: trembling hands, somber mien, dark and shadowed eyes, and he drank excessively."[87] Dorothy admired his ability to write, but she also felt sorry for him. One morning, after being up all night with her, he sent her to work in an open-air horse-drawn carriage and an hour later called her at the newspaper, saying, "Come back, I am lonely."[88] Presumably she had enough sense to ignore the invitation that morning and get her work done.

Work notwithstanding, Dorothy tried to be available to Gene (as she called him) at all hours of the day and night. When Tom Wallace closed at three or four in the morning, they often found another tavern that was still open. Sometimes she walked him home to his apartment, and after putting him to bed lay beside him under the covers, holding him close to keep him warm. "Dorothy, do you want to surrender your virginity?" O'Neill often asked her at moments like that, but she ignored the invitation.[89] In any case, he would be so drunk and exhausted that the idea was pointless.

O'Neill's love life was in crisis at this time (another reason why Dorothy felt sorry for him). The lady with whom he was in love had just left him, or more accurately had just been taken from him by the course of events. Louise Bryant, a slender and seductive brunette, had come under the spell of his plays and was attracted by his sullen look and shaking hands. With her large, dark eyes and parted lips, she knew how to meet his gaze with steady directness and "lightly run her fingernail down his arm", as Miller puts it.[90] The problem was that she was the mistress of O'Neill's friend and fellow writer, John Reed (who was also Dorothy's colleague at the *Masses* magazine), and while Reed had no problem temporarily sharing his mistress with O'Neill, he had no intention of giving her up permanently. Eventually Reed left the U.S. and, the couple having gotten married, Louise went with him, which meant O'Neill was pushed out of the picture.

(John Reed, who was the founder of the Communist Labor Party of America, went to Russia to write his book *Ten Days that Shook the Word*, a first-hand account of the 1917 October Revolution. Louise followed him and wrote numerous sympathetic articles about the Bolsheviks that appeared in newspapers across the United States and Canada. Both she and Reed continued to have relationships outside their marriage.)

Dorothy Day knew about the break-up between Eugene O'Neill and Louise Bryant, and she probably felt she could help fill the void in his life. She was not interested in a romantic relationship with O'Neill, but she wanted to help him. And she loved his plays. (Years later she claimed, with reason, that the character of Josie Horgan in O'Neill's play *Moon for the Misbegotten* was partly based on her.) But if Dorothy didn't have a romantic interest in Eugene O'Neill, there was another writer in the wings who did. Agnes Boulton, who by this time had become part of Dorothy's circle of friends, also spent a lot of time with O'Neill. When Dorothy drank with O'Neill in the Hell Hole, Agnes was frequently in their company too. And when O'Neill realized that Dorothy was not interested in romance, he inevitably turned his attention to Agnes. The two eventually got married and had two children together. After ten years of marriage, however, O'Neill left Agnes for the actress Carlotta Monterey.

The Hound of Heaven

The incident that seared itself indelibly into Dorothy Day's memory from her Greenwich Village days was none of the above, however. It was something more spiritual. One night, after putting down more than enough alcohol to cloud his eyes, Eugene O'Neill began to recite Francis Thompson's poem "The Hound of Heaven". His elbows resting on the table, chin cupped in hand, and looking at no one in particular, he recited the poem:

> I fled Him, down the nights and down the days,
> I fled Him, down the arches of the years;
> I fled Him, down the labyrinthine ways,
> Of my own mind; and in the midst of tears
> I hid from him.

Nobody was listening to O'Neill's drunken performance that night except Dorothy, and she felt the poem was speaking directly to her. In the following weeks, O'Neill repeated that poem many times at her request, his head downcast as he intoned: "And now my heart is as a broken fount, wherein tear droppings stagnate."[91] Rumor had it that he could recite the entire work from memory, all 182 lines of it. "It was one of those poems that awakens the soul, recalls to it the fact that God is its destiny," Dorothy wrote in *From Union Square to Rome*. "The idea of this pursuit fascinated me, the inevitableness of it, the recurrence of it, made me feel that inevitably I would have to pause in the mad rush of living and remember my first beginning and last end."[92]

By this time, Dorothy had become disillusioned with the Greenwich Village bohemians. Those talented writers, she came to realize, were drinking just "to fill the hole left in their lives when the theater went dark", and the glassfuls of alcohol they consumed gave them a phony camaraderie, a fake brotherhood.[93] More important, their interminable talk about feminism and world revolution was boring, as boring as the classes at the University of Illinois. Dorothy began to look for something deeper—in a Catholic church, of all places. The girl who had cursed God in college was now becoming a frequent visitor to Saint Joseph's Catholic church on Sixth Avenue, around the corner from the Golden Swan. (It was on the steps of that church that she found the two freezing men she brought to the Hell Hole for a stiff whiskey one night.)

After spending the whole night drinking, she often dropped into Saint Joseph's and knelt at the back while early morning Mass was in progress, not knowing what was going on at the altar, but warmed and comforted by the lights and silence and the atmosphere of worship. She noticed that some people liked to light a candle in front of a statue at the end of Mass, and she wished she knew how to do that. "What were they finding there," she wondered. "I seemed to feel the faith of those around me and I longed for their faith. My own life was sordid and yet I had had glimpses of the true and beautiful."[94]

But was her life all that sordid? Dorothy did not indulge in casual sex like the rest of the Greenwich Village set—not yet—and despite her drinking she worked hard, holding down a job as a reporter and supplementing that income with freelance writing. And her drinking wasn't as bad as some people said. Yes, the tough guys admired her ability to put down several belts of whiskey and remain sober, but Dorothy wasn't an alcoholic. Moreover, she didn't just write about the suffering of the poor. She contributed money to their causes and at times ate simple food in order to save extra money for those causes. One night she gave all she had to a collection and had to borrow money to pay for a taxi to get home.[95] And underlying that sensitivity to the poor was a longing for God, a long loneliness, that haunted her constantly, during her childhood, during her rebellious phase in college, during her drinking days in Greenwich Village.

Dorothy Day credited Eugene O'Neill and "The Hound of Heaven" with inspiring her to pursue that spiritual longing and not to be ashamed of it. "What I especially got from Eugene O'Neill was an intensification of the religious sense that was in me," she wrote later.[96] That religious sense had already been nourished by Dostoevsky's novels, and O'Neill reminded her of a character out of Dostoevsky. He was tormented by God and by death, and he coped with it by rebelling against man's fate. When O'Neill was living in Provincetown in Massachusetts, he used to swim far out to sea and "he played with the idea of death in those deep waters in the ocean from which all life springs", she wrote. What Dorothy saw in that was a reflection of her own struggle with God and with death, and for that reason "I owe him my prayers."[97]

A few years after Eugene O'Neill died (but while Dorothy Day was still alive), the Second Vatican Council addressed that same enigma, using much the same language. "Man is tormented not only by pain and by the gradual breaking-up of his body but also, and even more, by the dread of forever ceasing to be," the council said. "But a deep instinct leads him rightly to shrink from and to reject the utter ruin and total loss of his personality. Because he bears in himself the seed of eternity, which cannot be reduced to mere matter, he rebels against death."[98]

4.

Fatal Attraction

The Affair with Lionel Moise

It was spring 1918, and Dorothy Day's life had suddenly changed. No more late nights at the Golden Swan saloon; no more lying in bed till noon. Her work day now began at six in the morning, and the twelve-hour shifts were exhausting: changing dressings, removing bedpans, giving sponge baths and alcohol rubs. Just learning how to make a wrinkle-free bed was a chore, more difficult than writing a book review, she said.

Dorothy had made the surprising decision to enter the nurse's training program at Kings County Hospital in Brooklyn, where there was military-style discipline and high expectations for job performance. By evening she was so tired that she went straight to bed, and she seemed to never get enough sleep. She sometimes took a cold bath in the mornings because she was afraid she might fall back to sleep in a warm bathtub. The pressure was such that she began to skip breakfast in order to get the bed-making and morning baths finished by the 10 a.m. deadline. But as soon as the head nurse had finished the dreaded inspection, she slipped quietly into the kitchen where the cook fixed her some scrambled eggs and toast. The other student nurses did the same.

Difficult as it was, the discipline and structure of the hospital routine appealed to Dorothy after the meaningless winter she had spent in Greenwich Village. Her life now had a purpose. This was wartime, and there was a critical shortage of nurses and doctors in local hospitals because so many of them had signed up for military service. The stories of suffering and death that came from Europe were horrifying, and Dorothy wanted to do something to help. Anything! "Now that we are in the thick of war and there is so much work to be done, I might as well try to do some of it instead of sitting around playing at writing," she said. "And what is my writing now but book reviews, editing, toying with a novel of social significance? What good am I doing my fellow men?"[99]

By this time, the United States had finally entered the First World War. All through the early part of the war (from 1914 to early 1917), President Woodrow Wilson had remained on the sidelines, pursuing a policy of strict neutrality, and the US continued to trade with both sides. But that neutrality became more and more difficult to defend as Germany attacked ships in the Atlantic Ocean with their U-boats. The sinking of the *Lusitania*—a British passenger ship traveling from New York to Liverpool with hundreds of Americans on board—in May

1915 did much to turn the tide of American public opinion. By 1917, Wilson and the U.S. Congress had had enough, and in December of that year the U.S. entered the war on the side of the Allied powers. It was a decision that Dorothy Day strongly opposed. She was an uncompromising pacifist, and even the idea of becoming a nurse in wartime gave her pause at first. Would working at Kings County contribute to the war effort by freeing up more nurses and doctors to enlist for military service, she asked herself. She decided the answer was no and went ahead with her plans. "It's the poor that are suffering; I have got to do something," she said.[100]

In her autobiography *The Long Loneliness*, Dorothy described some of the difficult patients she attended in her new job. There was the ninety-four-year-old Canadian woman who objected to being bathed, saying that at her age she did not see why she had to be pestered with soap and water every day. Another patient threw things at the nurses. Her habits were so filthy that she was constantly in need of cleaning, but she spat at any nurse who dared to come near her. Then one afternoon, after a long day of cleaning up filth, this lady threw her bedpan on the floor, befouling Dorothy's shoes and stockings. She couldn't take it anymore. "I left the ward in tears, and sat in the washroom weeping uncontrollably at the ugliness and misery of life," she wrote. "I could not stop crying long enough to tell Miss Adams, so that my patients would not be left alone, but did the unforgivable thing and ran away, going to my room where I continued to cry."[101] The assistant superintendent of nurses eventually came to her room to console her and encourage her not to give up.

After that incident, she was transferred to the medical ward where there were fifty patients dying from influenza.[v]

The year 1918 was not just a year of brutal war. It was also the year of the Spanish flu pandemic, which lasted until mid-1920 and killed an estimated fifty million people, about three percent of the world's population at the time. The first wave of the flu began as Dorothy was beginning her work as a nurse probationer, and as the year progressed it got worse. By October, Dorothy was seeing eight to ten new patients a day, some collapsing as soon as they arrived, and dying by evening. At the end of the day, she and her co-workers had to wrap sheets around the dead bodies and send them to the morgue before handing over to the night shift. "When we came on duty in the morning, the night nurse was performing the same grim task," she said.[102]

A Reckless Infatuation

The minute Dorothy laid eyes on him she wanted him. It was his broken nose that attracted her, she told her sister Della. That nose gave him the tough-guy look that reminded her of a swash-buckling adventurer with a mysterious past. Unlikely as it might seem, she told Della, she had fallen in love, and she was shocked at the explosiveness of her feelings. Getting to know someone over a period of time and then feeling a physical attraction for

---

[v]   Dorothy did have a deep admiration for the nursing profession and called it "the most noble work women could aspire to". See *Long Loneliness*, p. 94.

him was one thing, she said, but "to see a man for the first time and want to … I'm ashamed of myself."[103]

Lionel Moise (pronounced Mo-ees) was an orderly who worked in one of the kitchen wards of Kings County Hospital to pay off his hospital bill. He had been found unconscious under an archway on Montague Street after a fight in a bar, and had ended up in the hospital more dead than alive; it took a week to stabilize him. A bunch of "dirty Mexican sailors" had put a drug in his drink, he said, and had taken all his money, which may or may not be true. Given Moise's well-known habit of drinking himself blind and then getting into fights, it is possible that he was the one who began the melee.[104] Presumably it was in one of those bar room brawls that he got the broken nose.

This was the man who "cracked her heart wide open", says Kate Hennessy. Dorothy was no longer "the unengaged and self-possessed woman she had been" in Greenwich Village, where her relationships were devoid of all romantic interest.[105] Now twenty years old, a reckless infatuation had taken hold of her, and she was resolute in pursuing the object of that infatuation. Most young women of her day would act the coquette in that situation—lightly run a fingernail down his arm, as William D. Miller would say—but Dorothy was not that type. She was much more direct. "You look just like Amenemhat III" she said to him when she bumped into him in the kitchen one morning. Surprised, he turned to look at her and asked "Who the hell is he?" One of the pharaohs of Egypt, she said.[106] (Dorothy had a postcard of Amenemhat on her wall.) Soon after that, she was seeking him out in a linen closet, or alone in the kitchen, and the two would embrace. Then she began to sneak out of her room in the nurses' quarters to meet him in a hidden part of the grounds, or in the park. "I am becoming a common little slut," the character representing Dorothy says in her autobiographical novel, *The Eleventh Virgin.* "I can't coordinate when you put your arm around me on the street—my knees wobble and I step on your feet."[107]

Lots of girls wobbled in the presence of Lionel Moise. "Big and blond with blue eyes, Lionel was a handsome—no, by all accounts he was beautiful—Jewish man who looked and acted like the fighting Irish and who loved to sing and write poetry," says Hennessy.[108] It was not just his physique but his knowledge of the literary classics and his talent as a writer that made him attractive. Moise had done a lot of different jobs (most recently as a cameraman with a movie crew in Latin America), but his most important identity was as a newspaperman. At the age of twenty-nine, he had already worked in the newsrooms of about ten major cities across the U.S., from New York to Boston, to Chicago, to Los Angeles and San Francisco, and he was remembered in those places as much for his personality as for his writing. Young reporters looked up to him, including a young Ernest Hemingway, who worked under him at the *Kansas City Star* in 1916. Yes, that newspaper had two colorful characters in the newsroom at the same time. One colleague, who knew the two of them well, said that Moise and Hemingway were "the only erudite rough and tough guys I ever knew. They could clean out a bar and then quote Shakespeare to the bartender." Friends who knew them both wondered if the rough and ready Moise had been not only a mentor to Hemingway but a role model as well.[109]

"Lionel was a great rewrite man," Hemingway wrote later. "He could carry four stories in his head and go to the telephone and take a fifth and then write all five at full speed to catch an edition. There would be something alive about each one. He was always the highest paid man on every paper he worked on. If any other man was getting more money he either quit or had his pay raised. He never spoke to the other reporters unless he had been drinking. He was tall and thick and had long arms and big hands. He was the fastest man on a typewriter I ever knew. He drove a motor car and it was understood in the office that a woman had given it to him. One night she stabbed him in it on the Lincoln Highway halfway to Jefferson City. He took the knife away from her and threw it out of the car."[110]

So it wasn't just the broken nose that attracted the usually cool, self-possessed Dorothy Day. She liked this man's explosive, uncomplicated personality and his undisciplined talent. He was a force of nature, an opinionated editor who didn't suffer fools gladly, and he was rumored to have once thrown a typewriter out the window in a fit of anger. He believed in a straight-forward, objective writing style that was built on the simple declarative sentence. No "stream of consciousness nonsense", he used to tell reporters.[111] [vi] Dorothy learned from that. But she also liked his down-to-earth philosophy. High-minded ideolo-gies and dreams about world revolution did not interest him. He simply "took the world as it was rather than suffer dismay with the world as it wasn't", Jim Forest said.[112] For Dorothy that was a refreshing change from the bohemian types she had met in Greenwich Village, who liked to debate the meaning of social

---

[vi] At one point, Moise noticed that she was reading James Joyce's *Portrait of the Artist as a Young Man*. He grabbed the book from her and threw it out the window of the train.

justice and sit around trying to explain the logic of free love using Freudian jargon.[vii]

Moise didn't have much patience with Freudian jargon. To him, Dorothy was just another young thing (he was ten years older than her) who was infatuated with him, and he let her know that he had no interest in marriage or children. "You should wait for some nice young man who will marry you … and give you babies … you know you love babies," he told her. Besides, "I have never had a virgin." But Dorothy refused to be put off or insulted. If anything, those words only fueled her passion and determination to seduce him. "Nothing you can say will hurt me," she said. "Nothing will persuade me to give you up. You're mine. I know it."[113]

Then one morning, he announced to everyone that he was leaving the hospital job and moving on. When he saw Dorothy's face turn white, he went over to her and said, "Poor child, I'm going to leave you." Her response came back like lightning. "No, you aren't … Come on out in the kitchen," she said. Out of the sight of others, they embraced, and he admitted he would miss her, but he intended to leave nonetheless. "What in hell would I do with a woman around?" he said. But she refused to be dismissed. "I can't live without you and I don't intend to stay here and suffer. You can run away all you want to, but I'll just run after you."[114] That afternoon, while Dorothy was alone in the linen closet, he came in to say goodbye and slipped a note into her bosom. It was the address of his apartment on

---

[vii] Moise was also part of the Greenwich Village circle, and biographers differ on whether it was there that Dorothy saw him for the first time, or in Kings County Hospital.

Thirty-Fifth Street. He had decided to take her with him after all, despite his protestations about freedom.

It was no surprise, then, when Dorothy left the hospital shortly after Moise did and moved in with him. In *The Eleventh Virgin,* she describes what happened when she arrived at his place on that first day. She got a cold reception because she didn't arrive on the day he expected her, but eventually his mood softened and he drew her to him. In his arms, the conflagration began, "the bright flame searing her, leaping up in her again and again until it was almost anguish".[115] She discreetly loses her virginity between two paragraphs in the novel.[viii]

But the conditions under which she moved in with Moise were surprising, not to say ironic. She was not to work or write, he told her, but only to be his woman. The financially independent feminist was now doing exactly what her Greenwich Village friends had said a woman should never do. She was giving up her career to become an obedient housewife with all the dedication that demanded: repairing clothes, darning socks, keeping the apartment clean, doing everything she could to please her man. At the same time, Moise kept reminding her that the arrangement was purely temporary. Commitment to a woman, he repeated, meant loss of his freedom. But "what does it matter," he said. "A month or two months, and it will pass and then I'll be free again."[116]

[viii] Although Pathé bought the movie rights for *The Eleventh Virgin,* it got mixed reviews in the press. A *New York Times* reviewer dismissed it as an example of the "truth at any cost" school of writing. See Forest, *Dorothy Day,* p. 65.

To add to the irony, Moise turned out to be intensely jealous when Dorothy glanced at other men. One night, in a restaurant with her old Greenwich Village friends (with whom she reconnected when she left the hospital), Moise noticed that Dorothy had casually put her hand on the shoulder of the man next to her while leaning over to talk to Peggy Baird. "I'll leave you here to embrace the gentleman on your right," he suddenly told her, getting up and heading for the door.[117] Dorothy was stunned. With no place to go, she spent the following couple of nights with Peggy, constantly weeping. Every time the phone rang, she hoped it was Moise calling to say he forgave her, but he made no contact. Then one night, while staying in another place, she attempted suicide by disconnecting the hose to the heater. Luckily a neighbor smelled the gas coming from under the door and saved her life. She made a second attempt by overdosing on drugs, but was again saved by friends.[118]

Moise did eventually take her back, and their relationship resumed, but then a new crisis crashed into her life. She discovered she was pregnant. She was afraid to tell Moise, but shared her agony with Peggy as she weighed her options, none of them easy. Going home was not a good idea, considering her relationship with her father, and going to a home for unwed mothers was too humiliating. Abortion seemed to be the only course. In any case, it would be the height of selfishness to bring a child into the world without "a fair chance of happiness", she told herself.[119] Peggy disagreed, saying that if only those conceived in ideal circumstances were allowed to be born there would be very few children in the world. Those words haunted Dorothy, especially when she looked at infants in baby carriages, or watched children playing in the park. Finally, she blurted out her dilemma to Moise. On hearing the news, he ordered her to terminate the pregnancy immediately, and that made up her mind. She sought the services of an abortionist.

The abortion procedure is described in painful detail in *The Eleventh Virgin*: the surgical instrument that cut the fetus from the lining of the womb, the painful contractions that came in waves every three minutes, the birth of Dorothy's child—dead. It is a graphic description and it put Dorothy in the company of a small number of avant-garde writers who dared discuss this subject openly. Most people didn't even whisper the word abortion in those days, let alone write about it. Neither did they write about female sexual desire.[120]

If *The Eleventh Virgin* is accurate, Moise had promised to meet her after the abortion procedure, but he never showed up. She waited for some hours and then went back by taxi to his apartment to find that he had moved out. In a note, he told her to forget him and expressed the hope that she would get "comfortably married to a rich man".[121] Along with the note was a little guilt money.

Marriage on the Rebound

A few months after her break-up with Moise, Dorothy did indeed marry a rich man, and one who was sixteen years older than her. Berkeley Tobey was one of the few members of the Greenwich Village set who had money, which made him an attractive catch for many young women. Dorothy was his fourth wife, and there were three or four after her. Nobody knew exactly how many times he got married. It was said that each time he picked up a new bride, he drove over to Connecticut for the marriage ceremony, but made sure not to consummate the marriage in that state, which meant that it was not valid. His other routine was to give each new wife a gift of the family silver, but when he got tired of her the silver mysteriously disappeared from the house.

In this case, however, the gullible one was Tobey, not Dorothy. She wasn't even remotely in love with him, but she married him for his money, and went with him on an eight-month-long honeymoon to Europe. They spent time in London (which reminded her of De Quincey and Dickens), and Paris (which reminded her of Hugo, Balzac and Maupassant). But Capri was her favorite. She loved Italian food, and she luxuriated in her afternoon naps on a yacht, or on a boat headed for Naples and the outdoor opera. For years afterwards, she wrote, "the taste of spaghetti and polenta and the sour wine brought me back to the months I spent beside the Mediterranean".[122] It was in Capri that she wrote her novel, *The Eleventh Virgin*, in which she used fictional characters to describe her painful affair with Lionel Moise. As her granddaughter pointed out, in Capri she found herself "married to a man she didn't love, writing about the man she did".[123]

As soon as they got back to the United States, Dorothy unceremoniously dumped Berkeley Tobey and avoided talking about the subject ever after. In *The Long Loneliness* she describes the trip to Europe at some length, but never mentions Tobey, or the marriage. She gives the impression that she was travelling in Europe alone. Years later, when a friend asked her why she misled her readers about her trip to Europe, she said: "About my marriage, I'll tell you more about it sometime. It lasted less than a year. I married a man on the rebound, after an unhappy love affair. He took me to Europe and when we got back I left him. I felt I had used him and was ashamed."[124]

But if the marriage with Berkeley Tobey was over, the affair with Lionel Moise was not. Back in the U.S., Dorothy immediately followed Moise to Chicago, where he had become the city editor of the *Chicago Post,* and the affair resumed. But it lacked the passion it had before, in part because Moise had other women and made no secret about that. Jobs were plentiful, though, and Dorothy had no problem finding work: a clerk at Montgomery Ward, an auxiliary at a public library, a cashier in a restaurant, a job with *The Liberator* (a radical newspaper that had moved from New York to Chicago), and finally a job at the *Chicago Post* that Moise arranged for her. By then Moise had lost his charismatic appeal. It was an act of violence that finally ended the relationship for ever. Moise held a gun to her head one day in a fit of jealous rage and, happy to be still alive, she immediately left Chicago and returned to New York. By then, according to her granddaughter, her weight was down to 108 pounds and, unsurprisingly for a woman of five feet ten inches, she looked emaciated. "I was scared," she told a friend. "I was glad to get away from him, but I was deeply in love with him."[125]

Writing years later, Kate Hennessy wondered how her grandmother could have been so infatuated with such an egotistical womanizer. "Lionel was a man on the run—from women, from jobs, from life," Hennessy wrote. No matter how you try to explain it, she said, you are left with an inescapable conclusion: Dorothy Day "was not always the clear-eyed visionary that we now see her as".[126]

That is indeed true, but it just highlights the wonder of Dorothy's eventual conversion to a life of faith. The mistakes of her youth were the raw material God used to eventually draw her to Himself. And others. For the rest of her life, Dorothy made it a habit of praying for Lionel Moise, as she did for Eugene O'Neill, and Mike Gold, and many others. These are examples of God's mysterious ways. The Hound of Heaven at work.

Two More Chicago Memories

Mae Cramer was another person who probably ended up on Dorothy's prayer list. Mae was a young Chicago prostitute who attempted suicide because things were not going well between her and her boyfriend. The boyfriend in question was none other than Lionel Moise. Yes, Dorothy and Mae had affairs with the same man, and both attempted suicide over him. Dorothy befriended Mae, and one night, when the two of them happened to be staying at a trade union boarding house, the police raided the place and put both Dorothy and Mae in jail; they assumed that both were prostitutes. Dorothy was eventually bailed out by her friends, and the case against her was dismissed, but she felt humiliated by the whole affair. This event was very different from her 1917 jail experience in Washington, D.C., when she had the status of a political prisoner and received a presidential pardon. Here she was incarcerated with prostitutes and, notwithstanding her respect for them as human beings, she felt branded and publicly smeared.

But, just as in the D.C. jail in 1917, she was shocked by what she saw behind those bars. "In the next cell to me," she wrote in *The Long Loneliness,* "there was a drug addict who beat her head against the bars or against the metal walls of her cell and howled like a wild animal. I have never heard such anguish, such unspeakable suffering." Being able to see that suffering close up made the Chicago jail experience worthwhile, she wrote, because "I was sharing, as I never had before, the life of the poorest of the poor, the guilty, the dispossessed."[127] That memory stayed with her.

Another Chicago memory that would stay with her was her growing affinity for Catholicism. Her occasional visits to a Catholic church, that began in Greenwich Village, became a habit in Chicago. She became a lunchtime visitor to the Cathedral there, even though the people she worked with were all militant atheists. That affinity was only confirmed when she rented a room in a household that turned out to be Catholic. The three women living there, all the same age as Dorothy, attended Mass every Sunday, and they gave Dorothy the feeling of missing out on something important: "They had their saints to pray to, I thought resentfully. I had nothing."[128]

Joris-Karl Huysmans' novel *The Cathedral*, which Dorothy read at this time, deepened her appreciation for Catholic architecture and made her more at home at Mass.[ix] But it was not just the architectural beauty that mattered. Dorothy noticed that it was in Catholic churches that she found the crowds of immigrants, most of whom were poor. That impressed her. Unlike her father, the proud Southerner who disliked foreigners, Dorothy was inspired by the simple devotion of these people and by

---

[ix] Huysmans's novel *The Cathedral* was one of a trilogy about a convert to Catholicism who became a Benedictine oblate. It is a detailed description of Chartres Cathedral in France. The other two novels are *The Return* and *The Oblate*. Dorothy read all three novels while in Chicago.

the faith that penetrated every corner of their lives. "Worship, adoration, thanksgiving, supplication—these were the noblest acts of which men were capable in this life," she wrote.[129] When a friend gave her a rosary as a gift, she treasured it even though she didn't know yet how to say the prayer.

Dorothy Day was being pulled in two directions at this time. She had one foot in the world of radical politics and free love, and the other in the world of Catholic spirituality and prayer. The tension between those two worlds, however, would not last much longer. A new affair in Dorothy's life would bring that tension to boiling point and force her to make a difficult decision.

Dorothy sitting at her desk, 1934

Dorothy in her senior years

Dorothy (center) at an anti-war protest, 1917

Dorothy seated with five grandchildren, circa 1958

Dorothy with Jacques Maritain (center) and
Peter Maurin (right), circa 1934

Dorothy with her partner, Forster Batterham, circa 1925

5.

The Choice Was either Forster or God

With Lionel Moise finally out of her life (in early 1924), Dorothy reconnected with her old friends in New York, Peggy Baird being at the top of that list. It was probably with Peggy and her new husband, Malcolm Cowley, that Dorothy stayed while looking for a place to rent. She always felt at home in Peggy's house, free to let her hair down, and that was exactly what she did one night. She seduced a total stranger and went to bed with him.

Biographer William D. Miller wonders what that one-night stand said about Dorothy's emotional state at the time. Was she just mindlessly playing around, like "romping kittens", enjoying "that brief moment of becoming one with someone else, of being held and loved?" That would be understandable considering the misery and despair she suffered during the previous five or six years. But there may have been more to it, Miller thinks. At this time, Dorothy desperately wanted a baby, so much so that it became an obsession. What worried her most was the abortion she had had while with Moise. Now twenty-six years old, she worried that she might be sterile as a result of that operation.[130]

One can assume that Peggy wasn't shocked by that one-night affair; she had probably done the same thing herself a few times. What did bother Peggy was Dorothy's reckless spending. By this time, Dorothy had a chunk of cash from the publication of *The Eleventh Virgin*, and she began to throw money around like a drunken sailor, wining and dining her old friends in expensive restaurants. Peggy wondered how long the money would last, and one day she suggested to Dorothy that she consider buying herself a cottage somewhere, a quiet refuge away from the crowds where she could do her writing. Dorothy loved the idea, and without delay the two of them were on the ferry to Staten Island in search of a suitable house. Before the day was over, they had found the perfect place, a fisherman's cottage overlooking the bay on the west end of the island where they could "watch ships moving slowly toward the Jersey shore".[131]

For the next four or five years, that cottage became Dorothy's dream hermitage by the sea, where "seagulls scream over the rocks … diving with a splash into the shallow gray water for a fish."[132] In her autobiographies, Dorothy described this place with her usual attention to detail, especially details in the lives of ordinary people. "Bait diggers come from miles around", she wrote, "old, gaunt, and weather beaten, most of them bending for hours over their digging forks, getting foot-long sand-worms and blood worms which they sell for fifty cents a dozen. Those quiet old men bring their lunches with them and seek out a sheltered spot at noon where they can eat and rest."[133] They let

Dorothy pick up the clams they dug up in the course of their work, and she took them back to her cottage.

The cottage itself was pretty basic, small and square with a tin roof and stovepipe chimney, but no electricity or hot water. There was a barrel stove in the corner in which she could burn the driftwood that was in plentiful supply on the beach. She immediately brought in comfortable chairs with a couch to furnish the place, and, of course, plenty of books. Her writing table faced the window where she had a view of the bay. "On the walls hung the fruits of our collecting," she wrote, "horseshoe crabs, spider crabs, the shell of a huge sea turtle … all picked up in little pools at low tide."[134]

A statuette of the Blessed Virgin, a house-warming gift Peggy gave her, was also part of the decoration. "She is dressed in the brightest of blue capes over a white dress with a golden girdle and golden bands around the neck and helm," Dorothy wrote. "She stands on a bright blue ball the same color as her cape and around the ball is entwined a snake, bright green with a pink and yellow apple in its red mouth."[135] Neither Peggy nor Dorothy were Catholics, but Peggy sensed that a gift like that would mean something to Dorothy. She was right. Dorothy called it her most precious possession. Peggy also helped her plan a garden for flowers and vegetables. Before they left the island that first day, Peggy had already sketched the outline of what a garden would look like. Dorothy soon became an enthusiastic gardener in her own right, and even secured a job writing a gardening column for the local newspaper, the *Staten Island Advance.* She also worked part-time for a real estate agent. The rest of the time she spent writing a novel, one that was never published, although it did appear as a newspaper serial.ˣ

Shortly after Dorothy bought the house on Staten Island, Peggy and Malcolm bought a house close by, and the three spent more time together. True to form, Peggy never worried much about how her house looked. The girl who was known for her messy apartment in Greenwich Village hadn't changed. It wasn't unusual for her to spend the whole day doing crossword puzzles, or playing solitaire, while dirty dishes were left piled up in the sink and the beds remained unmade. But Dorothy didn't care so long as she could use the bathtub. Their house had a water heater, which Dorothy's did not.

Always the outgoing type, Dorothy also spent time with her neighbors along the beach: immigrants from Italy and Belgium, a family of Russian and Romanian Jews, and in the nearby village some Irish people. Despite their difference in backgrounds, these neighbors all got along well. One of her favorites was a beachcomber called Lefty who lived without money because he was afraid he would spend it on drink. "Money is bad for me, I know it," he told Dorothy. "I can trade my fish and clams for fuel and food and what else do I need?"[136] Dorothy admired that kind of person.

ˣ The novel, called *Joan Barleycorn*, is about a woman who drank so much that her husband brought her to a desert island in the hope of curing her. The publisher rejected it, politely saying that it needed more work.

Forster Batterham

This was a happy time in Dorothy's life, and it wasn't just life at the beach that brought her joy. She now had a new boyfriend. His name was Forster Batterham, a mild-mannered man from South Carolina with a slight southern accent and a shy personality. In the presence of company, he didn't have much to say.

The rest of Forster's family, however, made up for his timidity. "The Batterhams were a long-lived, well-educated family of thinkers, writers, artists, and musicians, and they had children and grandchildren who also became well-educated thinkers, writers, artists, and musicians," says Kate Hennessy. Three of Forster's sisters had master's degrees, and Dorothy complained at times about being "unfavorably compared" to them.[137] Growing up in this clan (his parents were English-born), Forster was the exception. His college studies had been interrupted by the First World War, and he didn't go back to school when the war ended, much to the disappointment of his parents and siblings. He lacked ambition, they said. But Forster ignored them. Having grown up with seven sisters, he jealously guarded his freedom and independence. He earned just enough money to get by, which meant that he never spent money if he could avoid it. His main focus in life was doing what he loved most: fishing.

As soon as Dorothy met him, tall and lean, with a high forehead, sandy hair, and a passionate love for the outdoors, she was attracted to him. She knew he would love her beach house. "You simply must come down for a couple of days," she wrote to him from Staten Island. "There is plenty of room and plenty to eat, and plenty of room in the woods so you must get out. And if you don't I'll be coming back Monday. I miss you so much. I was very cold last night. Not because there wasn't enough covers but because I didn't have you."[138] Before long, they had agreed on a plan. Forster would spend the week in New York, where he had a low-paying factory job making gauges, and the weekends on Staten Island, where there was unlimited opportunity for fishing. Thus began what Dorothy called her common law marriage, but what Forster insisted was just a comradeship. Whatever one calls it, Dorothy was in love, and she could hardly stand it when they were separated. "I think of you much and dream of you every night", she wrote in one letter, "and if my dreams could affect you over long distance, I am sure they would keep you awake. I love you lots, sweetheart. Write soon."[139]

The attraction between Dorothy and Forster was in many ways the attraction of opposites, as William D. Miller points out. Dorothy was "vivacious, sociable, verbally expressive, literate, impulsive, and passionate seeker" while Forster was "the antithesis of all these things".[140] He was a poor conversationalist (Dorothy called him "Forster the inarticulate"), and he hated social life and avoided it. He didn't have much interest in books either; he read about one book a year. He did, however, read the *New York Times* faithfully, Dorothy said, "and all I knew of the political and foreign situation I knew from his reading aloud at the breakfast table."[141] His convictions about politics and social justice were as radical as hers.[xi]

[xi] The unjust execution of Nicola Sacco and Bartolomeo Vanzetti, Italian immigrants, in August 1927 in Massachusetts, deeply affected Forster. The case, badly tainted by anti-Italian prejudice, attracted world attention at the time. "Forster was stricken over the tragedy,"

Part of this attraction may have been Dorothy's penchant for befriending people who were different, people who were "misunderstood cast-offs", to use Miller's term.[142] Dorothy saw Forster's lack of ambition as something to be admired, not condemned. As she saw it, it was not that he lacked ambition, but that he refused to *be* ambitious like the rest of his family. Wealth and worldly success didn't impress him—or her! At the time, Dorothy was reading a book by American philosopher William James that decried the dehumanizing influence of greed and praised those who were detached from material things. The race to become rich has become so ingrained in modern society, James wrote, that one has to wonder if the old idea of "poverty as a worthy religious vocation" should not be revived as the "spiritual reform which our time stands most in need of".[143] In Dorothy's mind, Forster was an example of that reform.

William James would also have approved of Forster's love of the natural world. It was Peggy who sparked Dorothy's love for the beach, but it was Forster who helped her see it. He loved nature with a sensuous passion. He was also a gardener, and on weekends he rushed home from his machine-shop job in the city to check the vegetables with a flashlight. Influenced by Forster, the soil around the cottage became holy ground for Dorothy. The ocean was also a joy. One of their favorite recreations was taking walks together along the beach. They walked for miles together no matter how cold or rainy the day, "and this dragging

---

Dorothy wrote. "He did not eat for days. He sat around the house in a stupor of misery, sickened by the cruelty of life and men." Day, *Long Loneliness*, p. 147.

me away from my books, from my lethargy, into the open, into the country, made me begin to breathe. If breath is life, I was beginning to be full of it because of him."[144]

Along with this comradeship there was a happy sex life, although Dorothy was restrained when she talked about that in *The Long Loneliness*. She was more forthright in her personal letters to Forster. "Do you still want me or are you used to being without me?" she wrote while visiting her mother in Florida in September 1925. "However, notwithstanding, cold weather is coming, so fight as you may against it you'll have to sleep with me to keep me warm, and who knows in my luring night-gown, you might be seduced into doing something besides sleep. Huh?" Three days later she wrote this to him: "My desire for you is a painful rather than pleasurable emotion. It is a ravishing hunger which makes me want you more than anything in the world and makes me feel as though I could barely exist until I saw you again."[145]

Dorothy's Decision to Become a Catholic

It was on a beautiful June day in 1925 that Dorothy knew she was pregnant again. She, Forster, Peggy, and Malcolm went to a circus in Tottenville, a little town at the south end of Staten Island, and before the show they had lunch together. It was "wonderful fare", Dorothy remembered: dandelion wine and pickled eels, good home-made bread and butter, and afterwards root beer and popcorn while watching the show. Presumably that rich food produced the symptoms of pregnancy: nausea, fainting, and palpitations. "I will never forget my blissful joy," she wrote. "For a long time I had thought I could not bear a child, and the longing in my heart had been growing … I felt myself unfruitful, barren."[146]

It was at this time that Dorothy began to pray with more frequency. Her heart was filled with joy, and she felt the need to thank somebody—to thank God. Whether walking to the nearby village to get the mail, or strolling along the beach picking up driftwood for the stove, she repeated lines from the psalms, or from the Te Deum, prayers she had learned as a child in the Episcopal Church. She also began to use the rosary a friend had given her years earlier. She still had that rosary and, while she wasn't sure that she was saying it correctly, she kept on saying it because "it made me happy".[147] She also had the statue of the Virgin Mary that Peggy had given her, and she found herself gazing at it more and more as she moved around the house. On Sundays, she began to attend Mass in the local church, and she picked up some Catholic reading, including *The Imitation of Christ* by Thomas à Kempis and a biography of Saint Teresa of Avila.

But as Dorothy became more prayerful, she also found herself more conflicted. She remembered the professor in college who said that religion was a crutch for the weak, and the Marxist slogans about religion came to mind. "Prayer with you is like the opiate of the people," she told herself scornfully. "And over and over again in my mind that phrase was repeated jeeringly, 'Religion is the opiate of the people.'" But then something else occurred to her. She noticed that it was only when she was joyful that she prayed. She never prayed when she was feeling desperate. So how could religion be a crutch? If religion were a crutch, she reasoned, it would be in times of desperation that she would need it most. "And encouraged that I was praying because I wanted to thank Him, I went on praying," she said.[148]

Then another problem raised its head. Forster was uncomfortable with her interest in religion, and the more her interest grew the more uncomfortable he became. He was happy with life, he told her, and he saw no need to thank anyone—least of all God!—for that happiness. They began to argue about it, and the arguments led to long periods of tense silence as Dorothy pondered the irony of her dilemma. It was Forster's "ardent love of creation" that brought her to the Creator of all things, she said, but "when I cried out to him, 'How can there be no God, when there are all these beautiful things,' he turned from me uneasily and complained that I was never satisfied."[149] Dorothy *was* satisfied. That was precisely why she wanted to thank her Creator, but Forster couldn't understand that. Neither could he understand her enthusiasm about being pregnant. He did not believe in bringing children into a world that was so cruel and so unjust. He was not only against the institutions of religion. He was against the institution of marriage and family life. In sum, he was an anarchist and an atheist, he told her, and he was vehemently opposed to all the norms of society, be they from Church or state.

But Dorothy wanted the baby regardless. "My home, I felt, was not a home without one … No matter how much one was loved or one loved, that love was lonely without a child. It was incomplete," she said.[150] In December, she took an apartment in the city to prepare for the child's birth, and her sister Della came to stay with her. At age twenty-nine, with a history of gynecological problems since the abortion, she wanted to be sure nothing went wrong. Although not a person to frequent hospitals, she registered at a public clinic at Bellevue Hospital and began to make weekly visits there for examination. It was there, on March 4, 1926, that an ecstatic Dorothy Day gave birth to her daughter, Tamar. "When the little one was born," she wrote in *The Long Loneliness*, "my joy was so great that I sat up in bed in the hospital and wrote an article for the *New Masses* about my child, wanting to share my joy with the world.[xii] I was glad to write this joy for a workers' magazine because it was a joy all women knew, no matter what their grief at poverty, unemployment and class war."[151] The article, one of Dorothy Day's best pieces of writing, was picked up by dozens of workers' newspapers all over the world. Some four years later, while she was visiting Mexico, the painter Diego Rivera greeted her as the lady who wrote the famous article on childbirth. Her friend, Mike Gold, told her that even the Soviet newspapers picked up the piece, and that she had some rubles waiting for her in Moscow.

It was the birth of Tamar that finally pushed Dorothy into the Catholic Church. She wanted Tamar to receive the kind of religious instruction she had not had as a child. "We all crave order, and in the Book of Job hell is described as a place where no order is," she wrote. "I felt that 'belonging' to a Church would bring that order into her life which I felt my own lacked."[152] But where should she start? Whom should she talk to? The grocer and the hardware storekeeper were Catholics, also her neighbor down the street, but speaking to them about religion was difficult, even embarrassing. Finally, an opportunity presented itself one day when she saw a nun from the nearby convent walking down the road: "I went up to her breathlessly and asked her

---

[xii] The *New Masses,* for which Dorothy did occasional work as a free-lance reporter, was the successor of *The Masses*, which had closed several years earlier.

how I could have my child baptized."[153] Her name was Sister Aloysia Mary Mulhern, a no-nonsense Sister of Charity in her early sixties who had spent her life teaching in grade schools and was now taking care of babies in a large institution near Dorothy's beach house.

The nun's response to Dorothy's request was immediate and to the point: "How can your daughter be brought up a Catholic unless you become one yourself?" The result was a course of instruction that Sister Aloysia gave in Dorothy's cottage three times a week, during which Dorothy had to recite word for word the answer to each question in the Baltimore Catechism. If she stumbled in her answers, she was rebuked sternly by the nun. Years later, Dorothy described the kind of scolding the nun gave her during those classes: "And you think you are intelligent," she would say witheringly. "What is the definition of grace—actual grace and sanctifying grace? My fourth-grade pupils know more than you do."[154] No doubt the nun was right about that, Dorothy added with amusement.

Dorothy was determined not to debate points of dogma with Sister Aloysia, but to simply trust that light would come "as it sometimes did in a blinding flash of exultation and realization".[155] Meanwhile, Forster's resentment only grew. If he happened to be in the house when Sister Aloysia arrived, he would walk out and slam the door, and when Tamar was finally baptized (in July 1927) he refused to show up for the ceremony.[xiii] Following the church service, Dorothy put on "a delightful lunch

---

[xiii] Tamar was baptized in the Church of Our Lady, Help of Christians, Tottenville, Staten Island. Dorothy's niece and husband, who were Catholics, were her godparents.

of boiled lobsters and salad" at the beach house.[156] Forster was the one who caught the lobsters in his traps, but he refused to attend the lunch. He stayed away for several days.

It was becoming increasing clear to Dorothy that in order to become Catholic she would have to leave Forster despite her love for him. Their fights had become more frequent, and the tension in the house became so unbearable that it affected her health. When she developed breathing problems and was waking up at night with a choking sensation, the doctor concluded it was caused by stress. But the thought of leaving Forster was breaking her heart, and she kept postponing the decision. "I loved him for all he knew and pitied him for all he didn't know," she said. "I loved him for the odds and ends I had to fish out of sweater pockets and for the sand and shells he brought in with his fishing. I loved his lean cold body as he got into bed smelling of the sea, and I loved his integrity and stubborn pride."[157]

A particularly bad fight in December 1927 finally brought her vacillation to an end. Following the usual pattern, he walked out in anger and then returned a day or two later, but this time she said no. It was over, she told him. "It got down to the point where it was the simple question of whether I chose God or man," she wrote.[158] The following day she was baptized in Tottenville, in the church in which Tamar had been baptized some months before, and Sister Aloysia was one of the godparents. She received all three sacraments that morning, Baptism, Penance and Holy Eucharist, but she did so "grimly, coldly, making acts of faith, and certainly with no consolation whatever". Far from feeling the interior joy that one would expect, she was still conflicted, asking herself the haunting question: Was this authentic faith, or was she being fooled by "the opiate of the people?"[159] In her autobiography *From Union Square to Rome*, she describes her "miserable" journey that morning as she made her way from New York to Tottenville for the Baptism: "All the way on the ferry through the foggy bay I felt grimly that I was being too precipitate. I had no sense of peace, no joy, no conviction even that what I was doing was right. It was just something that I had to do, a task to be gotten through. I doubted myself when I allowed myself to think. I hated myself for being weak and vacillating. A most consuming restlessness was upon me so that I walked around and around the deck of the ferry, almost groaning in anguish of spirit. Perhaps the devil was on the boat."[160]

If the devil was on the boat that morning, he lost. Dorothy Day went ahead with her decision to join the Roman Catholic Church.

Begged Forster to Marry Her

This was not the end of Dorothy Day's relationship with Forster. He continued to visit her on weekends—to see Tamar if for no other reason—but Dorothy insisted that their love be platonic because they were not married. It was hard for both of them, and there seemed to be occasional slips when passion overcame them, but for the most part Dorothy succeeded in sticking to her resolution.[161] That became easier in late summer 1929 when she got a job away from Forster, in far-off Hollywood, California, writing film dialogue for Pathé with a salary of $125 a week. (They were impressed with a play she had submitted to Metro-Goldwyn-Mayer some months earlier.) Her contract there was for three months only, however, and when it expired she decided not to return to New York because she "hungered too much for Forster". She called him an occasion of sin.[162] Instead, in January 1930 she and Tamar headed for Mexico in a second-hand car—a Ford Model T—where she spent six months supporting herself by writing articles about Mexican Catholicism for the Catholic magazine *Commonweal*.

Meanwhile Dorothy and Forster continued to exchange frequent letters, thirty-three of which eventually became available to the public. In those letters, Dorothy pours out her thoughts and feelings in a very personal way, vacillating between feelings of passionate love for Forster and deep frustration at his pig-headed obstinacy. "I suppose you will sneer at me for writing to you but I can't help wanting to keep in touch with you some way," she wrote a few months after their break-up. "I suppose the best thing for both of us would be if you contracted an alliance with some nice fat Jewish girl (your ideal of beauty) even though I would be racked with jealousy if you did. I dream of you every night—that I am lying in your arms and I can feel your kisses and it is torture to me, but so sweet, too. I do love you more than everything in the world, but I cannot help my religious sense, which tortures me unless I do as I believe right."[163]

Some eighteen months later, she was still hoping she could talk him into marrying her. "Why don't you become reasonable or indulgent or whatever you want to call it and tell me to come back and marry you?" she wrote. "We could be so happy together. And even if we fought it would be better than this blank dead feeling. You know I love you and it isn't just loneliness which makes me long for you so." Six days later she wrote: "Do I have to be condemned to celibacy all my days, just because of your pig-headedness. Damn it, do I have to remind you that Tamar needs a father?"[164]

This correspondence went on for five years. Finally, on December 10, 1932, she sent him a letter that ended the relationship. But before she wrote those final words, she set the record straight about something that annoyed her. Apparently, Forster had said that she had become anti-sex and that that was the real reason she refused to be intimate with him. Dorothy sternly denied that. "Sex is not at all taboo with me except outside marriage," she wrote. "I am as free and unsuppressed as I ever was about it. I think the human body is a beautiful thing, and the joys that a beautiful body have are perfectly legitimate joys. I see no immediate difference between enjoying sex and enjoying a symphony concert." But the institution of marriage, she said, "has been built up by society as well as the Church to safeguard the home and children as well as people who don't know how to take care of themselves".

"You think this is only hard on you," she added. "But I am suffering too. The ache in my heart is intolerable at times, and for days I can feel your lips upon me, waking and sleeping … That is why I made up with you so many times, and went after you after we had had some quarrel. We always differed in principle, and now that I am getting older I cannot any longer always give way to you just because flesh has such power over me."[165]

She ended her letter with this statement: "I have given up hope now, so I won't try to persuade you anymore."[166] Dorothy meant it. Forster got no more love letters from her, and when their relationship resumed several years later it was as a friendship only. And even though she was free to marry in the eyes of the Church, she never did. Nor did she enter into a romantic relationship again. She described herself as a celibate. When in the late 1940s one of the Catholic Worker volunteers, Ammon

Hennacy, fell in love with her, she was quick to rebuff his sexual advances and put strict boundaries around their relationship. "I have a great love for you of comradeship but sex does not enter into it," she wrote to him. "When one is celibate, one is celibate. There is no playing around with sex."[167] At the same time, she insisted that it was the sexuality of her early years that led to the spirituality of her later life. She was thinking in particular of her passion for Forster Batterham. "The very sexual act itself was used again and again in Scripture as a figure of the beatific vision," she wrote in *The Long Loneliness*.[xiv] "It was not because I was tired of sex, satiated, disillusioned, that I turned to God. Radical friends used to insinuate that. It was because through a whole love, both physical and spiritual, I came to know God."[168]

The date of Dorothy's letter cutting off her relationship with Forster (December 10, 1932) is significant for another reason. Dorothy wrote that letter the day after she got back from Washington, D.C., where she had an intense spiritual experience, an epiphany that changed her life for ever. It is likely that the two events were connected. Dorothy would probably have broken up with Forster in any event, but her Washington epiphany gave her an added incentive. Dorothy Day's life was about to take a radically new direction, a direction that would make her a very famous Catholic and a saint in the making.

[xiv] "Beatific vision" is theological language for the face-to-face experience of God in Heaven which all Christians hope for. In that blessed experience, we believe, every human need and desire will be finally fulfilled.

6.

Peter Maurin

The Man Who Changed Dorothy's Life

On May 1, 1933, fifty thousand communists and trade union-ists crowded into Union Square in New York for the annual celebration of May Day. But there was little to celebrate at that time. The year 1933 marked the peak of the Great Depression in the United States, when the unemployment rate reached twenty-five percent and deflation was out of control. A third of U.S. banks failed, leaving millions of depositors penniless, while the surviving banks repossessed houses, shops, and farms because the owners could not pay their mortgages. The failures of capitalism were everywhere to be seen, and the united voice of the massive crowd boomed above Union Square in protest, singing the "Internationale", the official anthem of the socialist movement: "Arise, you prisoners of starvation / Arise, you wretched of the earth …"

Dorothy Day was one of those present that day, but she was not there to celebrate world socialism. She was there to sell the first issue of the *Catholic Worker,* an eight-page tabloid newspaper she had just founded with a small group of volunteers. Those who took the paper from her must have been bewildered by the name. A newspaper called the *Catholic Worker?* They were familiar with the *Daily Worker,* the communist publication that supported their right to unionize. Was this a Catholic version of the *Daily Worker?* Coming from an institution that was known for its anti-communist policies?

A Catholic version of the *Daily Worker* was exactly what Dorothy had in mind. This new paper, she wrote in the editorial, was addressing the same people the *Daily Worker* wrote for. Like the *Daily Worker,* she wrote, this newspaper was "for those who are huddling in shelters trying to escape the rain, for those who are walking the streets in the all but futile search for work, for those who think that there is no hope for the future, no recognition of their plight". The reader should know, she said, that the Catholic Church was not only interested in their spiritual welfare; it also had a program for their "material welfare", a program of social justice for the times in which they were living. "Is it not possible to be a radical and not an atheist?" she asked. "Is it not possible to protest, to expose, to complain, to point out abuses and demand reforms without desiring the overthrow of religion?"[169]

A Catholic version of the *Daily Worker* was indeed a novel idea, and what better place to unveil that new idea than in the midst of thousands of communists and socialists on May Day?

Actually, it was also a new idea for Dorothy herself. She was a convert to Catholicism, but for the first three years of her Catholic life she knew nothing about the social teaching of the Catholic Church. Lots of cradle Catholics were in the same boat, of course, as liberal theologians of her day liked to point out; the official stand of the Church on social justice was the best kept secret in Catholicism, they said. But while most cradle Catholics didn't have a problem with that lack of awareness (the question didn't even cross their minds), Dorothy Day certainly did. She loved the mystical side of the Church—the sacraments, the beauty of the liturgy, the lives of the saints—but she also admired the radicals and atheists who worked tirelessly to improve the lot of the poor, and she wanted to be involved in their cause despite being a Catholic. She wanted to do more than just sit on the sidelines and write about strikes and protests in Union Square. She wanted to be out on the picket lines, suffering the kind of abuse they were suffering. But that was not something Catholics did. At least, that was what she thought, and it troubled her deeply.

This crisis of faith came to a head in December 1932 when two prominent Catholic magazines, *Commonweal* and *America*, commissioned her to do a report on a hunger march that was scheduled to begin on November 30, 1932 in New York and travel to Washington, D.C. The plan of the organizers was to lobby for federal legislation that would protect the rights of workers (union rights we take for granted today). Unfortunately, the six hundred marchers who joined in this action were sponsored by organizations known to be communist sympathizers, and that didn't help their image in the mainstream press. All along the way to Washington, they were met by hostility from onlookers and law enforcement, as the newspapers stirred up fears of a "red revolution". In Wilmington, Delaware, the police used tear gas, clubbing the leaders and throwing some into jail. When they reached the edge of Washington, they were confronted by barricades across the highway that made it impossible to go any further. But the marchers refused to give up. For three nights they camped out in the bitter cold, and finally a federal judge sided with them, forcing the police to take down the barriers and let them go through.

As they got closer to the U.S. Capitol, the motley group left their cars and vans and walked the rest of the way. By then their number had grown to thousands, and to those who stopped to take a look they probably seemed more like a harmless horde of down-and-outs than the foot soldiers in a "red revolution". The security personnel at the Capitol did not see it that way, however. "There were riot drills of the Marines at Quantico; guards at the White House, Capitol, Treasury," Dorothy wrote in her article for *America*. Weapons available included machine guns, tear gas, night sticks, and lengths of rubber hose.[170]

In *The Long Loneliness,* Dorothy describes the last leg of the march and the anger it stirred within her. "On a bright sunny day the ragged horde triumphantly with banners flying, with lettered slogans mounted on sticks, paraded three thousand strong through the tree-flanked streets of Washington. I stood on the curb and watched them, joy and pride in the courage of this band of men and women mounting in my heart, and with it a bitterness too that since I was now a Catholic, with fundamental philosophical differences, I could not be out there with them. I could write, I could protest, to arouse the conscience, but where was the Catholic leadership in the gathering of bands of men and women together?"[171] Then she wrote this: "How little, how puny my work had been since becoming a Catholic, I thought. How self-centered, how ingrown, how lacking in sense of community! My summer of quiet reading and prayer, my self-absorption seemed sinful as I watched my brothers in their struggle, not for themselves but for others. How our dear Lord would love them, I kept thinking to myself."[172]

The following day was December 8, the feast of the Immaculate Conception, and Dorothy went to Mass at the Shrine of the Immaculate Conception in Washington (which was half built at the time). The bitterness of the previous day's march was still on her mind, and during that Mass she wondered why she was so unhappy with the official Catholic Church. After three years of Catholicism, she realized, her only contact with active Catholics was through the articles she was writing for Catholic magazines. She did not personally know a single Catholic layperson. Much as she loved some aspects of the Church, she said, she was "on the brink" of losing her faith.[173] "I offered up a special prayer, a prayer which came with tears and with anguish, that some way would open up to me to use what talents I possessed for my fellow workers, for the poor."[174]

Dorothy returned to New York the following day, December 9, and as soon as she walked into her apartment the answer to her prayer was siting waiting for her, although she didn't know it yet. His name was Peter Maurin. Years later, she would describe that Mass in Washington and the subsequent events as a life-altering climax, a turning point that would change her life for ever.

An Irish *Seanchaí* or a Holy Fool?

"I am Peter Maurin," the stranger said to Dorothy. "George Schuster, editor of *The Commonweal*, told me to look you up. Also, a red-headed Irish Communist in Union Square told me to see you. He says we think alike."[175]

The unexpected visitor was in his mid-fifties, dressed in a shabby suit that looked like he had slept in it (which he did), the pockets full of pamphlets and pages torn from books. He immediately launched into a monologue about Church history and social justice, quoting a variety of philosophers and saints, but Dorothy had just arrived back from Washington and all she wanted to do was give Tamara a hug and go to bed. She probably thought this man was just one more soapbox orator like those she had seen so often in Union Square, but this one was persistent. The following day he was back, talking incessantly and stabbing the air with his index finger to make a point, while she busied herself with house chores. Eventually, despite herself, she began to pay more attention to him. "Certainly I knew at once that he was French," she wrote. "It was difficult to become accustomed to his accent, which he kept although he had already been twenty years in America. He was intensely alive, on the alert, engaged in reading or in thought. When he talked, the tilt of his head, his animated expression, the warm glow in his eyes, the gestures of his hand, his shoulders, his whole body, compelled your attention."[176]

This was a soapbox orator with a difference. It was not just his animated personality that engaged her, but his ideas. Here was an active Catholic who was also a radical thinker. Here was a reformer who wasn't afraid to think outside the box, someone who could talk about religion and revolution in the same breath. Was that possible? Who was this man?

Peter Maurin was born in 1877 into a family of peasant farmers in the south of France who boasted that they had farmed the same piece of land for fifteen hundred years. He was one of twenty-three children, three of whom became nuns and three Christian Brothers. Like his male siblings, Peter was educated by the Christian Brothers and later entered that order, completing the novitiate program and teaching in their schools for a short time. But in 1902, he left the Christian Brothers and got involved in a movement called *Le Sillon* (the Furrow) that advocated Christian democracy and supported cooperatives and labor unions. They published a newspaper twice a week. But farming was in Peter's blood, and in 1909 he joined a stream of immigrants who were leaving for Canada where land was cheap and there was no military draft. He settled in Saskatchewan, where he lived the self-sufficient lifestyle of a homesteader until his partner was killed in an accident. After that, he wandered around the country taking any work he could find. Eventually he crossed the border (illegally) into New York State, where he continued to do whatever manual labor was available on the East Coast and the Midwest. He also gave classes in French. His many experiences included a short term in jail for hitching rides on freight trains. By the time Dorothy met him, in addition to teaching French for ten years, "he had dug irrigation ditches, quarried stone, harvested wheat, cut lumber, laid railway tracks, labored in brickyards, steel mills and coal mines."[177]

He never married, and he wasn't always an active Catholic. It may have been his job as a handyman at a Catholic boys' camp in upstate New York that brought him back to the Church.

He had worked in that camp for the five-year period before he met Dorothy, and his wages consisted of nothing more than his meals, a little pocket money, and a place to sleep. He shared the barn with a horse. But he had permission to use the chaplain's library, which meant more to him than money or luxury. By this time, Peter had not only returned to the Church, but had become a monk of sorts, filling each day with a balance of manual labor, Mass, meditation, and study. Whenever he got time off, he made his way to New York City and stayed in a flophouse in the Bowery for forty cents a night, while spending his day either in the New York Public Library or in Union Square expounding his ideas to anyone who would listen. The way to reach the man of the street, he liked to say, is to go to the street. Those who met him either loved him or ridiculed him as a holy fool, but that didn't bother him. "People say that I am crazy because I refuse to be crazy the way everyone else is crazy," he liked to say.[178] As Dorothy's granddaughter pointed out, he had taken his cue from the Irish *seanchaí* (pronounced *shan-a-key*), the storyteller who plays with words and speaks with a cadence in his voice. Peter's stories were like that. He used short, catchy phrases that commanded people's attention because of their humor and conciseness, and when he put those phrases on paper, they looked like stanzas of poetry. For example:

> The world would become better off
> if people tried to become better.
> And people would become better
> if they stopped trying to become better off.[179]

Dorothy's brother John called these collections of verses "easy essays", and the description stuck. Peter became famous for his easy essays.

It wasn't just the radicals and unemployed he met in Union Square who listened to him. Thomas Woodlock, editorial writer for the *Wall Street Journal,* was a friend of his. He and Peter had a common interest in the Thomistic idea of the common good, and Dorothy believed that Peter did indeed influence Woodlock's thinking as a writer. John Moody, head of Moody's Investment Services, was also a friend, as was Carlton Hayes, professor of European history at Columbia University. One day, the story goes, Peter went to the Hayes home to talk with Professor Hayes, but Mrs. Hayes thought he had come to fix some plumbing problem and asked him to take a seat in the basement. When the professor got home, he found Peter patiently waiting in the dusty cellar, not in the least offended.[180] As Dorothy wrote later, Peter was "a genius, a saint, an agitator, a writer, a lecturer, a poor man, and a shabby tramp, all in one".[181]

As soon as he met Dorothy Day, Peter knew she had potential. He had read her articles in *Commonweal* and *America,* and she reminded him of Saint Catherine of Siena, the medieval reformer and peace negotiator who had the ear of popes and princes. Dorothy could be a modern-day Saint Catherine of Siena, he thought. But he also knew that she was a new convert and had a lot to learn. Uninvited, he became a daily visitor to her apartment, giving her a crash course on the lives of the saints and the impact of their revolutionary insights on the Church of their time. "It is better to know the lives of the saints than the lives of kings and generals," he told her.[182] He also introduced her to contemporary Catholic thinkers such as Romano Guardini, G. K. Chesterton, Hilaire Belloc. Other favorites included Peter Kropotkin, the Russian anarchist, and Emmanuel Mourier, the guiding spirit of the French personalist movement. If Dorothy Day was a tireless reader, she had met her match in Peter Maurin. People called him a walking library.

The most impactful thing Dorothy picked up from this crash course concerned the Catholic Church's official teaching on social justice. Peter introduced her to *Rerum novarum,* Pope Leo XIII's 1891 encyclical on modern day labor in which Leo called on all Catholics to apply Christian principles to the problems of the Industrial Revolution. The encyclical—which Dorothy had never heard of— listed specific examples of those problems: the inhumanly long hours and exhausting work performed by laborers in the fields and factories; the widespread practice of child labor; the impossible conditions suffered by women in the workplace. The guilds of the Middle Ages no longer protected workers, the pope said, and the radical solution proposed by Marxists would only dehumanize workers further. He stressed the right of workers to organize, and called on Catholic workers to form their own unions.

Dorothy was exhilarated. This sounded just like something she would write herself. At last, she was getting an answer to the question that had haunted her while at Mass in Washington some weeks earlier, and it was coming from no less a person than a pope. Not only should Catholics be supporting marches like the one she was covering in Washington, but they should be out on the street leading those marches. And to add to her surprise, she learned that this papal encyclical was the first in a series of social justice encyclicals that came after Leo XIII's time—more documents she had never heard of. Pius XI's 1931 encyclical *Quadragesimo anno,* marking the fortieth anniversary of *Rerum novarum,* built on Leo's social teaching, and warned about the dangers to human freedom and dignity posed by unrestrained capitalism, socialism, and communism. John XXIII's 1961 encyclical, *Mater et magistra,* marking *Rerum novarum*'s seventieth anniversary, summarized the previous two encyclicals, and called for a better balance between the concerns of business and the rights of workers. Two years later, he wrote *Pacem in terris,* which further explored the rights of individuals in society. That was followed by Paul VI's 1967 encyclical *Populorum progressio,* which built further on the earlier encyclicals. (Since Dorothy's death, subsequent popes have continued this theme of social justice in their encyclicals.)[xv]

Peter's Three-Point Plan

But Peter wasn't just concerned with theory in books and papal encyclicals: he had a plan of action, a three-part program, he told Dorothy. The first part called for round-table discussions and lectures to make the encyclicals on social justice better known. He called this "clarification of thought", and he said it should be open to every point of view and school of thought. Second, houses of hospitality for the poor all over the country, ideally in every parish. Hunger and unemployment, he believed, was a spiritual problem, not a material one. If people would stop

---

[xv] Encyclicals on social justice published since Dorothy's death are: John Paul's *Laborem exercens* in 1981 and *Centesimus annus* in 1991; Benedict's *Caritas in veritate* in 2009; and Francis's *Laudato si* in 2015 and *Fratelli tutti* in 2020.

worshipping money and worship Christ, feeding the hungry, clothing the naked, and sheltering the homeless would follow naturally. Third, self-sufficient farming communities—he called them "agronomic universities"—where scholars and workers could live together on the land and concern for one's neighbor would be more important than one's bank account. In all, it was an ambitious program, and Dorothy wasn't sure what to make of it.

"Every day when I got home I found Peter waiting to 'indoctrinate' me," she wrote. "He stayed until ten when I insisted he had to go home. He followed Tessa and me around the house, indoctrinating. If we were getting supper, washing dishes, ironing clothes, or washing them, he continued his conversations. If company came he started over again from the beginning."[183] (Tessa was married to Dorothy's brother John. She and John were living with Dorothy and Tamar at this time.)

After some weeks of this indoctrination, Dorothy wanted to know where to begin. "Let's start with a newspaper," Peter said.[184] What he had in mind was mimeographed sheets he could hand out in Union Square, which didn't impress Dorothy. But the mention of a newspaper got her thinking. Why not start a real newspaper? After all, she had come from a family of journalists. Her father was a sports columnist. Her older brothers, Sam and Donald, had reputable careers as journalists too. And her young brother John (who now lived with her), had just secured a job with a newspaper. Besides, she had the experience of *The Masses*. Years before, she had put out the final edition of that publication on her own, at the age of nineteen. Dorothy now began to visualize the kitchen of her Fifteenth Street apartment as a makeshift editorial office and young John as her assistant editor.

But how would she pay for it? Peter had said not to worry about money, that God would provide, but that was easy to say. In the end, though, she decided to forge ahead not knowing whether the publication would be a weekly or a monthly. (It ended up being a monthly.) Father Joseph McSorley, a Paulist priest and friend, told her that their press could print 2,500 copies of an eight-page tabloid newspaper for only $57, cash in advance. It was a generous offer, but Dorothy didn't even have that much money. She had a couple of checks for articles she had written for magazines, but she needed those to pay bills. Then a friend donated twenty-five dollars, and the editor of a Catholic publication gave her another ten, followed by another ten from a priest in Newark, and one dollar from a nun. At that point, she calculated that if she delayed paying the gas and electric bill for a few weeks, she could reach the $57. "It was impossible to be with a person like Peter without sharing his simple faith that the Lord would provide what was necessary to do His work," she wrote later.[185] And so it was that she and John produced the first edition of the *Catholic Worker* newspaper on her kitchen table, and got it to Paulist Press in time for the launch date, the first of May 1933. The cost was one penny per copy.

The newspaper became an instant success among working-class Catholics. There were stories in every issue about strikes and the brutality adults and children faced when they dared walk in picket lines. Many strikers were beaten and tear-gassed, some even lynched, the paper reported. Peter's easy essays about the evils of the Industrial Revolution became a regular feature. Donations began to increase, and in a short time Dorothy was able to rent a former barber shop on the ground floor of her apartment building as a newspaper office. A communist admirer equipped it with used furniture, some of which was barely usable; Dorothy's desk was propped up with a Catholic encyclopedia because the leg was broken. A growing staff of enthusiastic volunteers soon formed around her as the newspaper's reputation grew. Many seminaries and parishes around the country began to order bundles, and within four months the circulation had grown to 20,000. Within two years it was 150,000. Dorothy and her volunteers were excited.

One of the volunteers, remembered fondly by Dorothy's granddaughter, was Big Dan Orr, an ex-policeman and unemployed truck driver who was "full of Irish wit and happiness." First thing in the morning he would come into the office and shout, "Is everybody happy?", to which all would laughingly respond "No!" Big Dan knew how to handle a horse and cart, so they rented the necessary equipment from a neighbor, and one of his jobs was to pick up the paper from the printer each month and deliver bundles to the parishes that were close by. As he drove the horse and cart up and down Fifth Avenue he loved to shout, "Read the *Catholic Worker!*." He called the horse Catholic Action, and he claimed that Catholic Action genuflected every time he passed Saint Patrick's Cathedral.

Meanwhile, Peter organized lectures and round-table discussions in the back garden, chaired by a professor from Fordham University. Jacques Maritain, the French philosopher, gave his first talk in English to that audience, but his French accent was so strong that nobody could understand him. Dorothy eventually became a close friend and admirer of Maritain and his wife, Raïssa.

The second part of Peter's program, houses of hospitality, evolved naturally in response to the needs of the neighborhood. It began with meals upstairs, in Dorothy's kitchen, for the volunteers and anyone else who happened to drop in at mealtime. Then they kept a large pot of soup and a pot of coffee on the stove all day, and the poor in the neighborhood began to come for refreshments and second-hand clothes. That prompted Dorothy to rent a cheap apartment nearby for homeless men: "a rat-ridden place, heatless and filthy, abandoned even by slum dwellers".[186] At eight dollars a month it was all she could afford, but her columns in the newspaper kept readers informed about their plans, and donation kept increasing. By the time the sixth edition had come out, she was able to rent an apartment to accommodate ten homeless women. Then she moved to a derelict house on Charles Street, on the outskirts of Greenwich Village, where there was room for everyone in one place: homeless women on the third floor, homeless men on the second floor, the newspaper offices on the first floor, and the dining room and kitchen in the basement.

Then came Mott Street, "glorious, miserable Mott Street, with its opera-singing Italian neighbors and Mussolini statues in the shop windows", Hennessy wrote. That two-building complex, which became the location of the operation in 1936, contained a total of thirty-six rooms. Dorothy's love of Italian food and culture meant that she was immediately at home in Little Italy, despite the admiration of so many for Mussolini. Unfortunately, conditions in the building were not much better than they had been in the previous places. As usual, it was rat-infested, "with garbage filling the halls and courtyard, and permeated with the smell of urine from the alley behind the building, a stench so powerful Tamar never forgot it".[187] (Tamar was ten years old when they moved there.) It had no heat, gas, or electricity. But with cleaning, painting, and a little creativity, the staff made it livable for the jobless men and women who came in for a bowl of soup, or a place to sleep. That Mott Street house served their needs for fourteen years before the operation moved to its present location, Saint Joseph House on East First Street.

The staff made a special effort to treat the homeless as guests, ambassadors of Christ, following the spirit of the Irish monks of old. Voluntary poverty was required of all staff members, following the spirit of Saint Francis of Assisi. They received only room and board, which could be a mattress on the floor, and pocket money. "We choose to spend the salaries we might be making if we were business-like on feeding and sharing our home with the homeless and hungry," Dorothy explained in a newspaper column. "We are willing to clothe ourselves in the donations of clothes that come in, we are willing to eat the plainest and most meagre of meals and to endure cold rooms and lack of privacy."[188] One staffer told of how surprised her family members were when they saw the slum conditions in which she was living and the shabby clothes she was wearing. But if visitors wanted to become volunteers themselves, they could do so with a minimum of formality. No interviews or forms to fill out, no orientation or probation periods. Just show up and do what needed to be done. Chop vegetables for the soup, serve the food, wash the dishes, distribute clothing, clean the toilets, take turns selling the *Catholic Worker* on street corners, or in Union Square.

The absence of bureaucracy was striking. The Catholic Worker house had no board of directors or organizational structure, no public relations desk, no glossy brochures, no ambitious grant proposals.[xvi] Dorothy never requested help from either the state or the Church, and she never had a savings account, or an endowment fund. She left the finances in the hands of God. Somehow it worked. The individual donations that came in from readers of the newspaper usually took care of the most pressing bills, and the rest had to wait till more money came in. "The wolf is not at the door", she wrote, "but he is trotting beside us. We make friends with him, too, as St Francis did. We pray for the help we need, and it comes."[189]

The third part of Peter Maurin's plan of action, what he called "agronomic universities", came from his love of cultivating the land. He called it his "Green Revolution". People would live on small self-sufficient farms, places of prayer and study, where laborers could become scholars and scholars could become laborers. In this, he was inspired by the monks of old who balanced manual labor with prayer and study, while at the same time providing hospitality to travelers and the poor. Peter was thinking of places like Ireland's Clonmacnoise, which became a famous center of scholarship and spiritualty, attracting seekers of enlightenment from all over Europe.[190] And it wasn't just in Ireland itself. Some of those monks, such as Colmcille and Columbanus, brought this monastic movement to Europe, and did so at a time when Europe needed it most, after the fall of the Roman Empire. Here is one of Peter's easy essays on that subject:

This made pagan Teutonic rulers
tell pagan Teutonic people

[xvi] Today, the structure of Catholic Worker houses varies according to the laws and requirements of each state.

"The Irish are good people
busy doing good."
And when the Irish
were good people
busy doing good,
they did not bother
about empires.[191] [xvii]

Dorothy Day did her best to implement this idea, first on a small experimental farm on Staten Island and then on a thirty-acre farm on a hilltop outside Easton, seventy-five miles from New York City. They later moved to a farm in Newburgh, sixty miles north of Manhattan, and then to one in Tivoli, New York State. From the beginning, the farms were a disappointment, however. Most of those who lived on them knew nothing about farming, and the ideal of scholars becoming laborers and laborers becoming scholars never became reality. The so-called scholars were city folk who were not interested in manual labor, while those who were willing to do manual labor resented having to carry the burden alone. The result was that the soil was often not tilled, the gardens were not weeded, and there was no effort to update the primitive farmhouses, or make them more livable. Even Dorothy's daughter, Tamar, who loved living on the land and was not afraid of manual work, had to adapt to conditions that were unnecessarily primitive.[xviii] In the early part of her

---

[xvii] For more on this see Thomas Cahill, *How the Irish Saved Civilization* (New York: Anchor Books, 1995), p. 171.

[xviii] Tamar grew up in the Catholic Worker movement and learned to love it. "It was exciting. I wouldn't have missed a moment of it," she

marriage, she and her new husband lived on the Easton ranch in a "tar-papered shack, twelve feet by thirty, cold in winter, hot in summer, with no electricity or running water, and they had to use an out-house next to the chicken coop".[192]

Some of the farms did, however, serve as venues for retreats and conferences. And they provided a peaceful refuge for staff members who wanted to get away from the noise of the city for a week or two.

A Face Set towards Eternity

Peter died on May 15, 1949, at the age of seventy-two, after a difficult period of physical and mental decline. The deterioration in his cognitive state was the most noticeable; the man who loved to play with language could no longer find the words to express himself. He was laid out for a day in the house of hospitality on Mott Street, and people came from all over to kneel and say a prayer. He was dressed in cast-off clothing that had been donated to the Catholic Worker, and because no rouge was used his face "looked like granite, strong, contemplative, set toward eternity",[193] His many priest friends, seminarians, lay friends, and staff celebrated a sung Mass (what was called a High Mass in those days) in the Salesian Transfiguration Church on Mott Street. "It was a loud and triumphant singing, with a note of joy", Dorothy wrote, "because we were sure Peter heard us in heaven; we were sure that angels and saints joined in."[194]

---

said. But as a child she found her mother's absence on long lecture tours difficult. See Margot Patterson, 'An extraordinary, difficult childhood', *National Catholic Reporter*, March 7, 2003.

L'Osservatore Romano, the Vatican newspaper, reported his death, as did *Time* magazine. He was a joyful Christian who had embraced poverty and the poor while trying to build up a society in which it was easier "for people to be good", *Time* said.[195] The Catholic Worker staff compared him to Prince Myshkin, the hero of Dostoevsky's novel *The Idiot*, who had no concern for personal appearance and saw the good in everyone he met. It was virtues like those that had earned Peter the nickname "holy fool", and the Catholic Worker volunteers were branded with the same label. They wore it as a badge of honor.

But the greatest tribute to Peter came from Dorothy herself. In answer to a 1954 letter from a student, Brendan O'Grady, who was doing a thesis on Peter Maurin, Dorothy wrote: "Peter Maurin is most truly the founder of the Catholic Worker movement. I would never have had an idea in my head about such work if it had not been for him. I was a journalist, loved to write, but was far better at making criticism of the social order than at offering any constructive ideas in relation to it. Peter had a program."[196]

According to Lincoln Rice, editor of *The Forgotten Radical*, there are more than 150 Catholic Worker houses of hospitality throughout the United States today, and some twenty-five in other parts of the world, including Australia, Argentina, Canada, England, Germany, Mexico, and Uganda. Of those, more than a dozen still experiment with farming communes.[197] Catholic Worker websites give slightly different statistics: 178 American communities and another 29 in other countries.[198] It is difficult to know the exact number because Catholic Worker communities are autonomous and don't report to anyone.

7.

Dorothy's Relationship with Her Bishop

Dorothy Day's political protests shocked many an old-fashioned Catholic over the years, but the action she took in March 1949 capped them all. She picketed the offices of Cardinal Francis Spellman, Archbishop of New York. For Catholics of her day that was like picketing God. Some must have wondered when a bolt of lightning would strike her down.

The cause of the uproar was a labor dispute in the Archdiocese of New York. The gravediggers at Calvary Cemetery had gone on strike for higher pay, but the cardinal, like many Cold War warriors of his day, believed the real issue was not pay but communist infiltration of labor unions. Because the gravediggers were unionized under the powerful Congress of Industrial Organizations (CIO), he refused to even meet with them. Instead, he brought in young men from the diocesan seminary to break the strike, and within a month it was over; the gravediggers had to return to work. Spellman had no regrets. He is reputed to have said that he considered his handling of the affair "the most important thing I have done in my ten years in New York".[199]

Dorothy Day would not agree. She got involved in the issue when some of the gravediggers showed up at the Catholic Worker house on Mott Street in need of assistance. She listened to their stories, decided that the strike was justified, and joined the picketers in front of the Chancery Office (behind Saint Patrick's Cathedral on Fifth Avenue). "I am deeply grieved", she wrote in a letter to Spellman, "to see the reports in the papers last night and this morning, of your leading Dunwoodie seminarians into Calvary cemetery, past picket lines, to 'break the strike' ... It is not just the issue of wages and hours as I can see from the conversation which our workers have had with the men. It is a question of their dignity as men, their dignity as workers, and the right to have a union of their own, and the right to talk over their grievances." She disputed the claim that the strikers were influenced by communists. Their union was solidly Catholic, she wrote.

The rest of her letter struck a conciliatory tone, however. She called Spellman "the outstanding Cardinal of the Church in America, a diplomat, a confidant and advisor of Pope and President", while the gravediggers were "little men", hardworking day laborers, but filled with their grievances. "And oh, I do beg you so, with all my heart, to go to them, as a father to his children. ... It is easier for the great to give in than the poor. ... Why cannot you go to the union, ask for the leaders, tell them that as members of the Mystical Body, all members are needed and useful and that we should not quarrel together, that you will meet their demands, be their servant as Christ was the servant of His disciples, washing their feet."[200]

It took quite a while for the cardinal's office to respond to this letter. Two years later, Monsignor Edward Gaffney, chancellor of the archdiocese, invited Dorothy to come to his office for a chat. At that meeting, Gaffney was gentle and friendly, but before the meeting ended he made a stiff request. Because the *Catholic Worker* did not represent the official policy of the archdiocese, he said, she should either cease publication or drop the word "Catholic" from the masthead. Dorothy said she would give the matter some thought and also consult other staff members. A few days later, she gave her response in a long letter that was respectful, but not the answer the chancellor was hoping for. She began by assuring him of her love and respectful obedience to the Church and "our gratitude to this Archdiocese which has so often and so generously defended us from many who attacked us". Then she got to the point. "All feel that the *Catholic Worker* has been in existence for eighteen years, since May 1933, under that name, and that this is no time to change it, so late in the day. I am sure no one thinks the Catholic War Veterans (who also use the name Catholic on their masthead) represent the point of view of the Archdiocese any more than they think the *Catholic Worker* does."

The *Catholic Worker,* her letter continued, had a worldwide circulation of 63,000 and was respected in reviews and journals all over the world: Australia, New Zealand, India, France, Germany, England, Ireland. "As I told you before", she wrote, "I could bring you a file of letters and clippings from many authorities, mostly clerical, which would show the value which has been put upon our work." Her criticism of capitalism, she reminded him, was no different from those expressed in the Vatican newspaper, *L'Osservatore Romano.* Shutting down a publication like the *Catholic Worker,* she wrote, would only put a formidable weapon into the hands of the Church's enemies. It would give fodder to the anti-religion voices in the world who try to prove there is no freedom of thought, or freedom of speech, in the Roman Catholic Church.

That did not mean that the *Catholic Worker* was perfect, she said. There were times when the pacifist views promoted by the paper could have been expressed more artfully. "I will admit that I personally am at fault in not being more careful as editor and censor," she said, promising that in the future the paper would be "less dogmatic, more persuasive, less irritating, and more winning".[201]

Apparently, her letter convinced the chancellor (and presumably the cardinal) to back off. The matter was dropped and Dorothy heard no more about it. "They didn't teach us in the seminary how to handle women like that," Spellman is reputed to have said.

Blind Obedience? No!

Dorothy Day took no pleasure in picketing Cardinal Spellman's office that time. Far from wanting to embarrass her bishop, she had a deep respect for his office, and she believed in the duty of obedience to Church authority. Before she brought out the first issue of the *Catholic Worker*, for example, she had planned on asking permission from the cardinal's office, but her spiritual director told her she did not have to. The editors of *America* and

The Sign told her the same thing "in no uncertain terms".[202] [xix] Nevertheless, she continued to believe that Cardinal Spellman had a say in what she published, even the power to shut her down. "I was quite ready to obey with cheerfulness if Cardinal Spellman ever told us to lay down our pens and stop publication," she wrote in one of her columns some years later.[203]

So how did she square that with the answer she gave Monsignor Gaffney? He had given her two options—either change the paper's name or cease publication—and she had chosen neither. How could she call that cheerful obedience? Her answer was simple. What Monsignor Gaffney gave her was a request, not an order, one he never followed up on, she said. Moreover, she was not writing anything that denied the faith, or in any way questioned the teachings of the Church. What her paper addressed was issues like labor relations, war and peace, the sins of capitalism, issues that Catholics of all stripes disagree on. Yes, there were experts at the highest levels of the Church who disagreed with the *Catholic Worker* on those issues, but there were also experts at the highest levels of the Church who agreed with her paper—including many popes.

Dorothy Day's understanding of her rights as a Catholic laywoman was pretty sophisticated. Cardinal Spellman was her chief priest and spiritual leader, she said, but he was not her ruler, nor did he pretend to be. "The Church has never told its flock that they have no rights of their own, that they ought to have no beliefs or loyalties other than those of the pope or one of his cardinals," she told Robert Coles. "No one in the church can

---

[xix] *The Sign,* for which Dorothy wrote occasionally, was published by the Passionists. It is no longer in existence.

tell me what to think about social and political and economic questions without getting a tough speech back: please leave me alone and tend to your own acreage; I'll take care of mine."[204]

Some critics were not satisfied with that answer, however, and pressed her further. What *if* the cardinal had followed up on the issue and ordered her to cease publication? What would she have done? Her answer: "First of all, I cannot conceive of Cardinal Spellman's making such a request of me, considering the respect he has always shown for freedom of conscience and freedom of speech. But in the event of so improbable a happening, I have said that I would obey. ... My faith that God will right all mistakes, mine, as well as his, would lead me to obey."[205] What she meant was that obedience to Church authority was, in the final analysis, a matter of faith in God, who had willed the existence of the Church in the first place. If she had to follow an order that she knew was a mistake, so be it. She would leave it in the hands of God, who knows how to write straight with crooked lines.

Dorothy Day's loyalty to Church authority, then, was not blind obedience. When she became a Catholic, she did so with her eyes wide open, fully aware that the Church was human as well as divine. That meant coming to terms with the mistakes Church leaders sometimes make. When one of her radical friends said to her that the Catholic Church was "a great, big, successful corporation, an international corporation", she cringed because she knew it was the truth—a partial truth, but an important one.[206] The comment haunted her for years. In fact, all her life, she said in *The Long Loneliness,* she lived "in a state of permanent dissatisfaction with the Church". She loved to quote theologian Romano Guardini, who once said that "the Church is the Cross on which Christ was crucified and who can separate Christ from His cross?"[207] When Robert Coles interviewed her for his biography, *Dorothy Day: A Radical Devotion,* she quoted those words of Guardini eleven times![xx]

What upset her most was the tendency of high Church officials to align "with property, with the wealthy, with the state, with capitalism, with all the forces of reaction".[208] There were days, she told Coles, "when I want to stop all those poor people, giving their coins to the church, and tell them to march on the offices of the archdiocese—tell all those people inside those offices to move out of their plush rooms and share the lives of the hungry and the hurt. Would Jesus sit in some big, fancy, air-conditioned room near the banks and the department stores where the rich store their millions and spend their millions?" Rather than feeling a sense of peace during Mass, she told Coles, "I feel like crying sometimes, or I flush with anger" at the Church's insensitivity to the poor.[209]

Despite her frustration with Church bureaucracy, however, Dorothy Day "never regretted for one minute the step which I had taken in becoming a Catholic". Why not? Because she made the distinction between the mystery of the Church and the frailty of those who run it. "It was ever in my mind", she wrote, "that human frailties and the sins and ignorances of those in high places throughout history only proved that the Church *must*

[xx] Fr Guardini (1885–1968) was a major figure in the Catholic Church of the twentieth century. He was the author of several books and a professor of philosophy and religion at several German universities. In 1968, Pope Paul VI offered to make him a cardinal, but he declined.

be divine to have persisted throughout the centuries. I would not blame the Church for what I felt were the mistakes of church-men"[210] (Day's italics). Peter denied Jesus three times, she liked to say. Moreover, not all priests and bishops acted like worldly bureaucrats. She knew many who lived up to her expectations, bishops and priests "who were poor, chaste and obedient, who gave their lives daily for their fellows".[211]

For Dorothy, what made it all worthwhile was the Church's prayer life. She loved the sacraments, especially the Mass, and the Liturgy of the Hours. She was faithful to weekly Confession in the tiny church of Our Lady of Guadalupe on West Four-teenth Street, and she loved reading the lives of the saints and the letters of Saint Paul. (Chapter twelve of Romans was her favorite.) For her, that was the side of the Church that mattered. "I love the church with all my heart and soul," she told Coles, "I never go inside a church without thanking God Almighty for giving me a home. The church is my home, and I don't want to be homeless. I may work with the homeless, but I have had no desire to join their ranks."[212]

Dorothy also believed in the Church's ability to reform itself. She had learned from Peter Maurin that the history of the Church was the story of constant efforts at renewal, periods of purification followed by periods of laxity followed by new periods of purification. *Ecclesia semper reformanda* is the Latin phrase theologians use for that. She considered Pope John XXIII one of those reformers, and when he published his encyc-lical *Pacem in terris* (1963) condemning the nuclear arms race, she joined an international group called Mothers for Peace who went to Rome to thank the pope for that encyclical.

Two years later, she was back in Rome for the fourth and final session of the Second Vatican Council, whose agenda included the completion of what was known as Schema 13, a proposed statement on war and peace. This time Dorothy was one of a group of women who had committed to doing a ten-day fast in support of that document. They hoped for a clear statement from the Council that would do three things: condemn all weapons of mass destruction; endorse non-violence as an appropriate way to fight for social justice; and express support for those who refused to do military service. Dorothy was not disappointed. She considered the final document, the *Pastoral Constitution of the Church in the Modern World* (*Gaudium et spes*), a vindication of the ideas she had been promoting all her life, in jail and out of jail.

Curiously, Dorothy also admired another papal reformer, one with a very different history from that of Pope John XXIII. Pope Celestine V had been the founder of a brotherhood of hermits and was a man of great holiness. But he had the misfortune of living in the thirteenth century, a time of exceptional corruption in the Catholic Church when the cardinals were steeped in the snake pit of European politics and were hopelessly divided into political factions. After spending two years trying to elect a new pope, those cardinals finally turned to this humble hermit in the hope that he would be successful in implementing the reforms the Church so badly needed. Unfortunately, it didn't work out the way they hoped. Celestine was out of his depth and lasted only six months. Faced with the wealth, worldliness, and political entanglements of the papacy—which prayer and fasting seemed powerless to untangle—he resigned. For Dorothy, that story was a cautionary tale, an important reminder of the constant need for reform in the Catholic Church.

It was Ignazio Silone, one of her favorite authors, who introduced her to Pope Celestine's story. Silone's play about that pope, *The Story of a Humble Christian*, fascinated her; but Silone wrote a novel about the Church that impacted Dorothy even more. Called *Bread and Wine*, it is one of Silone's most famous novels, and it became one of Dorothy's most treasured books during the Catholic phase of her life.

Bread and Wine

Ignazio Silone (his real name was Secondino Tranquilli) was born into a peasant family in the village of Pescina in central Italy in 1900. When he was sixteen years old, he witnessed an earthquake that killed some fifty thousand people in a matter of minutes and left unspeakable destruction in its wake. The rich in the area immediately packed their things and moved out, as apparently did many of the priests. As Silone saw it, the poor were left to bury their dead, abandoned by the Church at a time when they were most in need of the sacraments.

Silone eventually escaped the devastation in order to complete his education, but he never forgot the landless peasants like his family, "poor people whose capacity for suffering and resignation had no real limits".[213] Driven by outrage over the exploitation of those peasants, he got involved in socialist politics at an early age and in 1921 became a founding member of the Communist Party of Italy, eventually becoming a covert leader with direct ties to Moscow. After some years of social activism that included arrests and jail time, he was exiled by the Mussolini government.

Before long, Silone became disillusioned with the betrayal and murder he saw in the Communist Party of Russia, as he began to realize that the promise of Marxist liberation was nothing more than one tyranny taking the place of another. While at a meeting in Moscow, he refused to sign a denunciation of Leon Trotsky without being able to see the text, and the communists expelled him. He settled in Switzerland, gave up his socialist activism, and spent the rest of his life writing novels and short stories that tirelessly preached political rebellion. He died in 1978. His fiction, full of anecdotes about the oppressive nature of fascism, became a beacon of hope for many as they witnessed the rise of the communists, the Nazis, and the fascists before and during the Second World War.

Bread and Wine, a very Catholic novel about a very Catholic country, was Silone's most autobiographical work, and of all the books Dorothy Day read during the Catholic period of her life this one seems to have been the most influential. She read it four or five times, she told Robert Coles, and he saw her eyes tear up when she read excerpts from it aloud. Coles said that Dorothy was at her most open and forthright "during those moments when she had *Bread and Wine* near her—when she was under its spell."[214]

The novel, which is set in Silone's native Abruzzo, fictionalizes Salone's own disillusionment with the Catholic clergy of his youth. But it is more than that. It fictionalizes his disillusionment with promises of liberation, whether from Church or state, left or right. The hero of the novel, Pietro Spina, a political radical who is on the run from the fascist police, goes underground, putting on a black cassock and disguising himself as a Catholic priest with the name Don Paolo. As the story unfolds, Don Paolo becomes a saint in the eyes of the poor (who think he is a real priest). Crowds begin to come to him for Confession, which puts him on the spot as he tries to find excuses for why he cannot hear Confessions. He tells them he belongs to another diocese and does not have faculties to hear Confessions in the Abruzzo diocese. But the crowds continue to come anyway. Don Paolo turns out to be more priestly than the priests themselves.

Eventually, the clerical cassock becomes more than a disguise. Almost despite himself, Pietro Spina begins to interiorize the identity of a priest, or at least the values a good priest should represent. He had long since left the Church, of course, but now he finds himself returning to his Catholic roots in search of answers to a fundamental question that has haunted him: How can he reconcile the worldly quest for social justice with the otherworldly quest for eternal peace in Heaven? It is a quandary that haunted not just the fictional character in the novel, but the author himself. "Two encompassing visions held the imagination of Ignazio Silone," says American literary critic Irving Howe, "the secular promise of socialist liberation and the Christian promise of spiritual transcendence." For Silone these two visions are always in tension, and the result is a deep discord in the human heart, a "conflict between the need for action and the desire for contemplation, the one striving for worldly power and the other a straining towards individual purity".[215] In *Bread and Wine,* Salone presents those opposing visions as an inevitable fact of life, and he makes no effort to reconcile them, or offer a solution to the quandary. But neither does he conclude from this that life is meaningless, or absurd. He continues to believe in the possibility of human progress.

This optimism is dramatized well in Chapter 18 of the novel when Pietro Spina goes to see his old friend Uliva, who was living in Rome at the time. Pietro and Uliva had been members of the same communist cell when they were students, but Uliva had long since left the movement and is now living in poverty. Pietro is shocked by the squalid living conditions in which he finds his old friend, but he is even more shocked by the cynicism and despair he hears in his voice. After spending ten months in prison for shouting "Long live liberty" in the Piazza Venezia, Uliva says, he spent years sleeping under bridges and on the steps of churches "with my jacket rolled up under my head as a pillow". Pietro urges him not to give up the struggle, not to capitulate. "We must remain united with the workers' cells," he says. But Uliva responds with a personal attack. He accuses Pietro of becoming a revolutionary out of fear, forcing himself to believe in progress because the opposite terrifies him.[216]

Saddened by Uliva's bitterness and despair, Pietro finally leaves. Later that day, he gets the news that Uliva has just died in an unexplained explosion in his apartment (the apartment Pietro had visited that morning). When the firemen come to clean up the rubble, they find detailed plans for blowing up a church. Uliva had planned to carry out a terrorist attack during a church service that was to include government officials. Pietro is shocked by the news, but the tragedy only confirms his conviction that there must be more to life than this despair and death. That was also the author's personal conviction. The novel is autobiographical. Like Pietro Spina, Ignazio Silone himself persistently refused what Irving Howe calls "the lure of nihilism".[217] For all his disillusionment with revolution, he continued to be an optimist.

It is not surprising that this novel would appeal to someone like Dorothy Day. The irony of a fake priest being more real than the real priests wasn't lost on her. But that wasn't her only focus, or even her main focus. After all, she had read about worse clerical problems in the thirteenth century when Celestine V was pope. Her main focus was the wider human problem that haunted Silone; the tension between the promise of socialist liberation and the Christian promise of transcendence. Like the fictional Uliva, Dorothy became disillusioned with the promises of Marxist liberation, and like Uliva she experienced the despair that that disillusion can bring. Her time in jail in Washington, D.C., in November 1917 was an example. "I had no sense as I lay there of the efficacy of what I was doing … I had an ugly sense of the futility of human effort, man's helpless misery, the triumph of might. Man's dignity was but a word and a lie. Evil triumphed."[218]

But unlike Uliva, Dorothy didn't succumb to that despair. On the contrary, the despair became a step on her road to finding an answer. When faced with the choice between socialist liberation and the promise of transcendence, she chose transcendence. In other words, she became a Catholic despite the Church's failings. In the end, it came down to a stark choice: either God or despair, either the folly of the Cross or nothingness.[219]

But Dorothy's struggle wasn't over yet. During her first few years as a Catholic, the tension between transcendence and socialist liberation continued to trouble her because she was unaware of the social justice teaching of the Catholic Church. She felt that in becoming a Catholic (choosing transcendence) she had abandoned the poor (socialist liberation). As described in the last chapter, this struggle came to a climax while covering the 1932 hunger march in Washington as a reporter, when she found herself standing on the sidelines as an onlooker when her real desire was to be out in the street marching with the protesters. At that time, she offered up a fervent prayer, "that some way would open up for me to use what talents I possessed for my fellow workers, for the poor".[220] That prayer was answered when she met Peter Maurin. For the first time, she began to realize that she could be a believer in life everlasting *and* be an activist for the poor. The promise of transcendence and the promise of socialist liberation were finally reconciled.

8.

An Activist Who Was Rooted in Prayer

In April 1957, Dorothy Day took a thirty-six-hour bus ride to the U.S. South on a mission that had particular importance for her. She wanted to give moral support to the Koinonia community, an interracial farming cooperative in Georgia that had come under brutal attack from white terrorists who were trying to put the operation out of business.

Founded by a Baptist minister, Koinonia (the name is Greek for communion or fellowship) consisted of six people, black and white, who lived on a thousand-acre chicken farm a hundred miles from Atlanta. They shared the fruits of their work in common, and for fifteen years they had operated in relative peace, an example of what was possible even in the segregated South, but then hostile neighbors began a campaign to destroy them. In addition to boycotting their products, they dynamited one of their roadside stands, cut their barbed wire fences, set a barn on fire, and shot at their houses from cars speeding by. "I have seen the marks of gunshot in the houses," Dorothy wrote.[221] She stayed for a week and wrote a series of letters to the Catholic Worker community describing the "terror of the night" that gripped the residents every time they saw the headlights of a car pass by on the road.

On the third night, Dorothy and another woman volunteered for the night watch, which meant sitting in a station wagon by the roadside, under an oak tree, with a floodlight turned on. Her companion whiled away the time that night singing hymns and playing an accordion. Dorothy, for her part, took out her breviary and began to quietly pray Matins, and as she did so she thought about the Trappist monks at Holy Ghost monastery, Georgia, not far from where she was.[xxi] Those monks were also up at that unearthly hour, praying that same prayer. Suddenly a car approached and shots rang out as the attackers peppered the station wagon with bullets, barely missing the two women. Dorothy was badly shaken by the experience. But when she wrote about it in the following issue of the *Catholic Worker*, her focus was to express her admiration for the courage of the Koinonia members, not the barrage of bullets that could have killed her and her companion. Whether Koinonia survived or not, she wrote, this should be a model for the future. (Koinonia did in fact survive, and is still flourishing in Georgia today.)

[xxi] Trappists is a common name for Cistercians of the Strict Observance.

Her Breviary

When Dorothy pulled out her breviary in the station wagon that night, it wasn't out of fear, or out of a need to kill time. Even if she wasn't doing a night watch under that Georgia oak tree, she would have prayed from that breviary, although probably at a later hour in the morning.

The Breviary is the prayer that punctuates the hours of the day for priests and religious and some laity—Vigils (or Matins) at dawn, Lauds later in the morning, Vespers in the afternoon, and Compline at bedtime—and Dorothy was faithful to that daily routine in her later years. (Today we call it the Liturgy of the Hours.) It was the Trappist monks in Georgia who opened up the beauty of that prayer regimen for her. By this time, she had become a regular visitor to Holy Ghost Monastery because one of the volunteers at the Catholic Worker, Jack English, had entered that monastery with the religious name Brother Charles; she went to visit him after her stay with the Koinonia community.[xxii] Dorothy modelled her prayer life on the daily rhythm of manual labor and prayer that she saw in that monastery. But she also found time for some traditional devotions, in particular the Rosary. That was the prayer she turned to when she couldn't sleep. Robert Ellsberg, who knew her better than most, estimates

---

[xxii] Dorothy's connection with the Trappists continued to widen. A friendship of letter-writing eventually grew between her and Fr Thomas Merton, and when she purchased the building in Lower East Manhattan (what is now Maryhouse), the Trappist community of Rochester donated $100,000. She was buried in a casket made by the Trappists.

that the time Dorothy spent in prayer each day came to at least two hours. "In all her activities, even as she marched on picket lines or went to jail, she was strengthened by a constant discipline of prayer," he says.[222]

That didn't mean that prayer was always easy. Like all mortals, there were times when she was plagued with distractions despite her best intentions. "My mind like an idiot wanders, converses, debates, argues, flounders," she wrote while on a sabbatical in 1943. "If I get in fifteen minutes [in a day] of honest to God praying, I'm doing well."[223] On another occasion, after a solitary retreat, she put it this way: "Sometimes I prayed with joy and delight. Other times each bead of my rosary was heavy as lead. My steps dragged, my lips were numb. I felt a dead weight. I could do nothing but make an act of will and sit or kneel, and sigh in an agony of boredom."[224]

Nevertheless, Dorothy continued to pray, and she expected the staff at the Catholic Worker to do the same—lest they become "an empty cistern unable to help others".[225] Mass was part of the daily schedule for those living in the community (she was always able to find priests willing to celebrate Mass), and the day always ended with Compline, prayed together. Some visitors to the soup kitchen—those with a secular mindset—expressed surprise at this emphasis on prayer and wondered why more time wasn't devoted to addressing the roots of poverty in society. Dorothy quickly dismissed that criticism because she had heard it all before. This was precisely the question she resolved during her early years as a Catholic: how to balance the tension between the promise of transcendence and the promise of social liberation (discussed in the last chapter). It was her study of the papal encyclicals that convinced her that Catholics should be pursuing both of those promises at the same time. In other words, they should be living lives of prayer *and* working to eliminate poverty. Dorothy practiced that balance for the rest of her life, and when critics accused her of "wasting" too much time on prayer she gave them a blunt answer. Working for social justice causes, she told them, can be an empty and meaningless task if one does not have a strong faith in God, who rights all wrongs in His own time, regardless of human effort. Furthermore, even if all hunger and want were somehow abolished from the earth, there would still be poverty—spiritual poverty!

"I am convinced that prayer and austerity, prayer and self-sacrifice, prayer and fasting, prayer and vigils, prayer and marches, are the indispensable means ... And love," she said.[226] And if that made her sound like an impractical dreamer, so be it. We *are* impractical, she told Robert Coles, "as impractical as Calvary", and we gladly call ourselves fools for Christ. "If an outsider who comes to visit doesn't pay attention to our praying and what that means, then he'll miss the whole point of things ... We are here to bear witness to our Lord. We are here to follow his lead."[227]

Those pious words, let it be noted, came from a radical who was not afraid to use non-pious tactics when the situation called for it. Dorothy's Day's presence on picket lines was legendary, whether it was protesting the Vietnam War, or supporting the action of a labor union she admired. Even the Archbishop of New York didn't escape her anger when he refused to negotiate with the gravediggers at Calvary cemetery. Those confrontations were Dorothy Day's way of addressing the roots of poverty, but they were not a priority for her. She called them "morality in the abstract". What filled most of her days were acts of kindness to individuals, what the Catechism calls the corporal works of mercy: giving a cup of soup to an alcoholic on the street, or patiently listening to the incoherent babble of a mentally ill down-and-out who came to talk to her. Those acts of kindness, Dorothy kept saying, were more important than the political movements we join to address the roots of poverty. In fact, those acts of charity are the key to how God will judge us.[228]

But that way of life demanded perseverance. Some days, she told Coles, she spent the whole morning chopping vegetables for soup and the whole afternoon sitting with a mentally ill unfortunate in the outpatient department at Bellevue Hospital, and by the end of the day she wondered how much longer she could go on doing work that showed so few tangible results. It was her faith in the Cross that kept her going. "We must suffer for those we love", she wrote in her autobiography *From Union Square to Rome*, "we must endure their trials and their sufferings, we must even take upon ourselves the penalties due their sins. Thus we learn to understand the love of God for His creatures. Thus we understand the Crucifixion."[229]

The Retreats

The in-house problems at the Catholic Worker were neverending: pressure from creditors looking for their money; fights between mentally disturbed people on the daily breadline; clashes of personality among staff members. It fell to Dorothy to make the hard decisions these problems demanded, and it took its toll on her. "I pray for love—that I may learn to love God, and I am surrounded by such human hatred and dislike that all natural love and companionship is taken away from me," she wrote in her diary in March 1945. "Love in practice is a harsh and dreadful thing compared to love in dreams."[230] xxiii

Dorothy needed a break from this pressure, and she finally found it in Baltimore, in days of recollection that were given by a Canadian Josephite priest, Pacifique Roy, who shared her convictions about the poor. Dorothy was so enthusiastic about this priest's talks that she invited him to give a week-long retreat to all the Catholic Worker staff, using the farm in Easton as the location. She sent an invitation to all the Catholic Worker communities—the movement had by now grown to thirty houses of hospitality and eleven farms—and, to her satisfaction, representatives from practically all the houses showed up. That retreat became an annual exercise, but rather than using Father Roy she soon turned to a younger priest he recommended, Father John Hugo of the Diocese of Pittsburg, who used the same retreat model as Father Roy. Both priests got their retreat notes from Father Onesimus Lacouture, a Canadian Jesuit who had given this retreat to thousands of priests and laity in Canada and the U.S. It had become a significant spiritual movement in its own right. What distinguished this retreat from others was its strict demand for radical conversion in one's life, and it often included all-night vigils and strict fasting. For Dorothy it marked a new chapter in her spiritual journey, and began a forty-year friendship with Father Hugo, who would have a profound impact on the Catholic Worker movement and on Dorothy herself. She

---

xxiii The description of love as "a harsh and dreadful thing" is a quotation she borrowed from the saintly Father Zossima in Dostoevsky's novel *The Brothers Karamazov.* Dorothy quoted those words frequently in her writing and talks.

took that retreat more than twenty times over the years, most of the time given by Father Hugo.

Hugo's message, based on the Lacouture notes, was simple and direct. Holiness was not something reserved for those who live in monasteries, he said. All have an obligation to strive for holiness. All have an obligation to take the Sermon on the Mount literally. He lamented his own years in the seminary when (he claims) he never once heard mention of the call to holiness. "That call, we were led to believe, was reserved for religious, for whom it was also often mistakenly regarded as only a counsel."[231] Father Hugo preached complete detachment from all material things. The best thing to do with the best of things in your possession is to give them away, he said. The coat hanging in your closet on a winter day belongs to someone who is freezing on the street, he said, echoing the early fathers of the Church. Give it away. Do without it.

Words like that fired the soul of Dorothy Day, who heard echoes of what Peter Maurin called the "shock maxims" of the Gospel. "This was what I was looking for," she said after the first retreat. "I saw things as a whole for the first time with a delight, a joy, an excitement which is hard to describe. This is what I expected when I became a Catholic." [232] Dorothy was comparing these retreat talks to the sermons she had been hearing on Sunday mornings, which were sometimes little more than the pastor's pet peeves, or an appeal for money.

Not all Catholics were as enthusiastic as Dorothy about Father Hugo's rigorism, however. Many found his talks too extreme, too negative, more likely to discourage the average Catholic than to inspire sanctity. Those critics pointed in particular to his talks on the beatitudes. Father Hugo had rewritten that passage from Matthew's Gospel so that the eight blessings became eight condemnations. Blessed are the poor in spirit became a condemnation of those who put their hearts in earthly riches. Blessed are the meek became a condemnation of those who depended too much on bodily comforts. Dorothy's own daughter, Tamar, was among those who found this too much. "It could lead people to despair for fear that they wouldn't get into heaven," she said, "and it created a rift in the Worker between those who had made the retreat and those had not, between those who had given up smoking and those who had not."[233] But Tamar did admit to one good outcome. The retreat caused Dorothy to finally give up her two packs of cigarettes a day.

Eventually, Father Hugo's superior, Bishop Hugh Boyle, asked him to refrain from giving retreats and concentrate on parish ministry. It was an order Hugo meekly accepted, reminding friends that unless the grain of wheat falls into the ground and dies it bears no fruit. Father Lacouture was also silenced by his Jesuit superiors. Privately, Dorothy Day continued to defend both Father Hugo and Father Lacouture, pointing out that their retreats were no more demanding than what one would find in the writings of Saint John of the Cross. Any retreat that does not make Catholics examine their consciences is a failure, she said. "For too long, too little has been expected of us. We were learning how to die to ourselves, how to live in Christ, and all the turmoil of the movement, all the pruning of natural love, all the disappointment were explained by the doctrine of the Cross, in the folly of the Cross."[234]

Father Hugo was eventually reinstated by Bishop Boyle's successor, Bishop (later Cardinal) John Dearden. Dorothy took her last retreat from Father Hugo in 1976, four years before her death. Father Lacouture was never restored to teaching by his superiors, but he was allowed to minister to Indigenous people in Canada at the end of his life. Dorothy went to visit him during that painful period of his life, and she was the only American to attend his funeral in Quebec in 1951.

I Could Have Written Another Book

Controversy notwithstanding, the importance of the Lacouture–Hugo retreats in Dorothy Day's spirituality cannot be overstated. A meeting she had with William D. Miller in April 1975 illustrates this. By this time, Miller had become Dorothy's close friend and official biographer, and she wrote a letter to him requesting that he visit her while she was taking a break in the beach cottage on Staten Island.[xxiv] The letter commented on a book she was reading, but then added an enigmatic statement. "With your help I could have another book with little effort."[235] She didn't explain what she meant.

Miller did come to visit her, and on the first day she took him on a tour of familiar places on the island, all of which brought back memories of her past. She was in a nostalgic mood. On the second day, when they met more formally in the cottage, her mood was more tense. "She seemed to be suffering. Her face was white and drawn, and most of the time her gaze was directed at something far away," Miller said.[236] In the course of the conversation, she gave him a copy of her autobiographical novel, *The Eleventh Virgin,* and said that the principal events in

---

[xxiv] This was not the fisherman's shack Dorothy owned when she was young. That building had burned down years earlier.

that book, including the abortion, were true. A few minutes later, she pointed to two boxes of notes and articles on the floor. She had thought of burning those boxes, she said, but decided not to. Instead, she asked him to take them and do whatever he thought best with them. Burn them if he thought that would be best, she said. Miller said he would burn nothing. He would go through the material, piece by piece, and put it in the Catholic Worker archives at Marquette University.

Among the materials Miller later found in those boxes was a collection of three hundred pages of handwritten notes, entitled "All is Grace", that Dorothy had put together during her retreats over the years. Miller eventually learned that this was the raw material for a book that Dorothy hoped to write, but never did. For nearly forty years, she had struggled with that book, searching for a way to tell her readers how the retreats had helped her, how God had "lifted her out of the bottomless pit of despair into which her life had once fallen".[237] But she could not get that story down on paper. Miller concluded that this was what she was referring to when she made that enigmatic statement: "With your help I could have another book with little effort."

The result was that Dorothy felt misunderstood all her life, frustrated by critics who said the Catholic Worker people "had their heads way up in the clouds" and were too focused on prayer.[238] And when those critics praised her—as they frequently did—they did so despite her life of prayer, not because of it. In the words of Mark and Louise Zwick: "They applaud Dorothy's activism, her life with the poor, her amazing stand for truth in the face of criticism on all sides in regard to pacifism, but do not recognize its spiritual base."[239] Father Hugo was more blunt: "There would be later friends and co-workers who would be ignorant of this history of the retreat, would pass it by, speak slightingly of it, or even deny it."[240] Such critics, Hugo said, preferred to see her through the secular mystique of activism rather than rooted in a life of prayer. Hugo called Dorothy Day "a contemplative in action, an authentic mystic in the Catholic tradition".[241]

Heroes from the Past

Dorothy didn't have far to go to find inspiration in that mystical tradition. She found it in the lives of the saints, holy men and women who were revolutionary figures in their day, Church reformers who stubbornly refused to accept things as they were and often paid a price for it. Those heroes from the past became Dorothy's intimate companions. "There are days when I've not talked much to anyone who is alive, but I've talked plenty to people who once were alive and now have departed for the sight of God," she told Coles.[242] Saint Joseph was one of those. She had a large statue of him in the entrance to Saint Joseph House in Lower Manhattan, and she put the unpaid bills at the foot of that statue to remind him that he was in charge of finding the money.

The variety of saintly characters she quoted was amazing. Michael Garvey, in his foreword to *On Pilgrimage*, gives an example. In January 1948, Dorothy was so busy that she made very few entries in her journal—only nine for the whole month. But even in those few journal entries, she managed to mention nine saints: Saint Angela of Foligno, Saint John of the Cross, Saint Teresa of Avila, Saint Agnes, Saint Francis, Saint

Catherine of Siena, Saint Paul, Saint Martin, and Saint John Bosco. Mixed among those names were writers who happened to cross her mind: the Brontë sisters, Charles Dickens, Father Garrigou-Lagrange, Ignazio Silone, Hilaire Belloc, G. K. Chesterton, Arthur Koestler, Aldous Huxley, and Martin Buber.[243]

One of her favorite saints was someone who was not revolutionary in the usual sense of that word. Thérèse of Lisieux was a nineteenth-century Carmelite nun who lived her brief life (she died at twenty-four) within the walls of an obscure cloister and never did anything famous. Dorothy loved her so much that she wrote a book about her, the only completed biography she ever wrote. What she loved about the Little Flower (as she was called), was the simplicity of her spirituality, her "little way," her conviction that the most insignificant things we do each day can be turned into prayer. "Paper work, cleaning the house, dealing with the innumerable visitors who come all through the day, answering the phone, keeping patience and acting intelligently", all of those things can be turned into prayer, Dorothy wrote in one column.[244] She saw this as a spiritualty for the common man, a path to sainthood for people who don't feel worthy of great acts of heroism. That "little way" eventually became a guiding policy for the *Catholic Worker* newspaper. Jim Forest remembered going through back issues of the paper and seeing a banner headline on the front page of one issue that said: WE ARE ALL CALLED TO BE SAINTS. It was cast in the kind of bold lettering that a daily newspaper would only use for the assassination of a president, or the outbreak of war.[245]

When admirers applied the description of sainthood to Dorothy herself, however, she was quick to deflect the comment with humor. "Don't call me a saint," she liked to say. 'I can't be dismissed that easily." That was her way of handling a compliment that she found uncomfortable. She did not mean by those words that real saints could easily be dismissed. She was referring to unreal saints, the superhuman images that were created by some saccharine writers of the past.

In her personal life, Dorothy did not worry about whether or not she was a saint. She worried about her sins, in particular the sin of pride. Was she just trying to make herself "feel good" when she fed those hundreds of people, she asked herself. Did she get a swelled head when people told her that the pope admired her and that one day she would be a saint? "The sin of pride, I keep repeating to myself, is the worst of all sins, and it lurks around every corner," she told Coles.[246] A visiting nun put it even more bluntly. Feeding the poor is "dangerous work", she told Dorothy, because you begin to think you are "God's gift to humanity". Dorothy was caught off guard by the comment, but she never forgot it. "I'll remember her words until my dying day," she said.[247]

There was another sin from the distant past that seemed to hang over her in silence—the abortion she had in her twenties. Those who knew Dorothy well sensed that she was haunted by that decision all her life. It was the one thing she rarely talked about, or wrote about. One has to assume it was too painful to bring up.

Epilogue

As Quiet as the Turning of a Page

"We shall be stripped," Dorothy Day liked to tell people, stripped of mobility, of independence, of privacy, of memory, finally of breath itself.[248] She got that statement from a talk on death given by Father Hugo, and she made it a pillar of her own spiritual life. But Dorothy wasn't always that detached or graphic about the end of life. It only came after years of struggle.

Her fear of death started when she was eight years old. "I began to be afraid of God, of death, of eternity," she wrote in *The Long Loneliness.* "As soon as I closed my eyes at night the blackness of death surrounded me. I believed and yet I was afraid of nothingness. What would it be like to sink into that immensity?"[249] Even at that young age, she was asking questions about where we humans end up. "Life would be utterly unbearable if we thought we were going nowhere, that we had nothing to look forward to," she wrote at that time.[250]

It was only when she embraced Catholicism that her search for the meaning of life and death finally came to an end. By then, it had come down to the stark choice described in Chapter 7: either the folly of the Cross or a life of despair. It is no accident that Dorothy Day became an admirer and close friend of fellow converts Jacques Maritain and his wife Raïssa, who faced the same choice. As students in Paris, they made a vow to end their lives if they did not find a satisfactory explanation for the apparent meaninglessness of life. Like Jacques and Raïssa, Dorothy opted for the Cross rather than despair, and the words she later used to describe that option are striking, even jubilant. "Now the creed to which I subscribe is like a battle cry, engraved on my heart. Now I can say: 'I know that my Redeemer liveth and in the last day I shall rise out of the earth.'" [251] It was that confident faith in the afterlife that enabled her to speak so candidly about being slowly stripped of mobility, of independence, of privacy, of everything.

In her particular case, however, that stripping began sooner than she had expected. In her late sixties, Dorothy was forced to cut back on her grueling speaking schedule because of arthritis and an enlarged heart that caused frequent shortness of breath. The doctor gave her medication that helped, but after a mild heart attack in 1976 she never drove a car again. By 1978, her walk was slow, and she had trouble keeping her train of thought. "I've been ill—please pray for me," she wrote to her old friend, Sister Peter Claver. "Flu, exhaustion after a heart attack months ago—cannot seem to get my strength back. Can't make the retreat this year … Also a feeling of jittery nerves! Shaking and trembling inside."[252]

Dorothy spent those declining years in Maryhouse, the Catholic Worker house on East 3rd Street in Lower Manhattan, a neighborhood that brought back a half century of memories.[xxv] It was in that area that she lived when she was acting editor of *The Masses* at the age of nineteen. It was around there that she spent many nights pub-crawling with Eugene O'Neill, often walking him home when he was drunk and tucking him into bed. Memories of Mike Gold must have flooded her mind also, and the many nights they spent together, sitting on the piers overlooking the East River and talking into the early hours of the morning about Tolstoy and world revolution. And Saint Joseph's church! It was there she went early one morning after a night of drinking at the Golden Swan, not knowing what was going on at the altar, but warmed and comforted by the lights and the silence.

Now she was almost eighty-three years old, confined to her room on the second floor, unable to go downstairs even for Mass. She was brought Communion each day, before which she spent a half hour in preparation and after which another half hour in thanksgiving. "My job now is to pray," she said.[253] As the memories kept coming back and she reflected on the life God had "given" her, she tried to put her thoughts on paper one last time, but she realized that her writing days were over. She had been stripped. "I was going to try to make a summary for myself, write what mattered most—but I couldn't do it," she told Robert Coles. "It will soon be over."[254] Her daughter Tamar came to stay with her over Thanksgiving that year, sensing that

---

[xxv] Maryhouse, a place for homeless women at 55 East 3rd Street, is still there today. Her room is kept exactly as it was when she lived there.

she did not have long to live. On Thanksgiving Day, she ate almost nothing, and the following two days were not any better. She was so weak she could barely get out of bed to go to the bathroom. Finally, on Saturday afternoon, God took her into eternity. Only Tamar was in the room at the time. It was a death as quiet as the turning of a page, Jim Forest said.

The following day her body was laid out in an unvarnished pine coffin, donated by the Trappists, and was placed in the Maryhouse chapel where visitors came to pay their respects, kneel for a prayer, and share memories in an adjacent room. That stream of visitors continued into the night. The next day, Dorothy's eight grandchildren carried the coffin to the Church of the Nativity, a half block away, where Cardinal Cook stood at the entrance waiting to bless the remains. The crowd at the funeral Mass was huge and varied: some rich, some poor, some Catholic, some of other faiths, some who believed in nothing. Among those present was Forster Batterham, the crusty old atheist who had vowed never to darken the door of a Catholic church. According to Jim Forest, he even went up to receive Communion, something that would not have impressed the religiously strict Dorothy.[255] Only active Catholics are allowed to approach the altar with that intention.

But Dorothy would have been happy at Forster's presence nonetheless. By the end of their lives, she and Forster had become good friends and communicated almost daily. She had long since accepted his partner, Nanette, with whom he had lived for thirty years, and she even helped nurse Nanette when she died a slow death from cancer in 1960. The day before Nanette departed this world, she asked to be baptized. It was Dorothy's saintly example that motivated her.

Dorothy Day is buried in Resurrection Cemetery on Staten Island, walking distance from the fisherman's cottage where she made that blessed decision to become a Catholic at the age of thirty. The marker on her grave is a simple rectangular stone, low on the ground, with the words:

Dorothy Day
November 8, 1897—November 29, 1980.
Deo Gratias

Thanks be to God indeed!

A Dorothy Day Chronology

Born November 8, 1897

Arrested outside White House and jailed, November 1917

Publication of *The Eleventh Virgin*, 1924

Bought cottage on Staten Island, Spring 1925

Tamar born, March 4, 1926; baptized July 1927

Dorothy baptized, December 28, 1927

Prayed at Shrine of Immaculate Conception in Washington, D.C., met Peter Maurin, December 1932

First issue of *Catholic Worker*, May 1, 1933

Newspaper circulation reached 100,000, early 1935

Publication of *From Union Square to Rome,* 1938

Attended first retreat with Father John Hugo, August 1941

Picketed Cardinal Spellman, Archbishop of New York, March 1949

Publication of *The Long Loneliness*, January 1952

Two-part profile in *The New Yorker*, October 1952

Sentenced to thirty days in jail for defying civil defense drills, July 1957

Joined ten-day fast in Rome during the final session of the Second Vatican Council, September–October 1965

Catholic Worker house moved to present location, Saint Joseph House, 36 East First Street, July 1968

America magazine devoted entire issue to mark her 75th birthday, and Notre Dame University awarded her the Laetare Medal, November 1972

Spent ten days in California jail for picketing vineyards with Cesar Chavez, August 1973

Invited to address the Eucharistic Congress in Philadelphia, suffered heart attack soon after, August 1976

Received 80th birthday greetings from Pope Paul VI, November 1977

Mother Teresa visited her at Maryhouse, New York, July 1979

Died at Maryhouse, November 29, 1980

Endnotes

1   Jim Forest, *All Is Grace: A Biography of Dorothy Day* (Maryknoll, New York: Orbis Books, 2011), p. 258.

2   Forest, *Dorothy Day*, pp. 257, 258.

3   I Corinthians 2:19.

4   Mark and Louise Zwick, *The Catholic Worker Movement: Intellectual and Spiritual Origins* (Mahwah, New Jersey: Paulist Press, 2005), p. 247.

5   Zwick and Zwick, *Catholic Worker*, p. 248.

6   William D. Miller, *All is Grace: The Spirituality of Dorothy Day* (New York: Doubleday, 1987), p. 35.

7   See Dorothy Day, *Selected Writings: By Little and By Little,* ed. Robert Ellsberg (Maryknoll, New York: Orbis Books, 1992), p. 277.

8   Quoted in Jim Forest, *All Is Grace: A Biography of Dorothy Day* (Maryknoll, New York: Orbis Books, 2011), p. 307.

9   Quoted in Forest, *Dorothy Day*, p. 308.

10 Quoted in Forest, *Dorothy Day,* p. 306.

11 Quoted in Forest, *Dorothy Day,* p. 313.

12 Liam Stack, "Was Dorothy Day Too Left-Wing to Be a Catholic Saint?", *New York Times*, January 21, 2022.

13 Quoted in Forest, *Dorothy Day*, p. 7.

14 Quoted in William D. Miller, *Dorothy Day: A Biography* (San Francisco: Harper & Row, 1982), p. 4.

15 Quoted in Forest, *Dorothy Day,* p. 4.

16 Quoted in Forest, *Dorothy Day,* p. 168.

17 Dorothy Day, *The Long Loneliness: The Autobiography of Dorothy Day* (New York: HarperSanFrancisco, 1952), 26.

18 Kate Hennessy, *Dorothy Day: The World Will Be Saved by Beauty: An Intimate Portrait of My Grandmother* (New York: Scribner, 2017), p. 4.

19 Dorothy Day, *From Union Square to Rome* (Maryknoll, New York: Orbis Books, 2006), p. 25.

20 Quoted in Forest, *Dorothy Day,* 13.

21 Day, *Long Loneliness*, p. 30.

22 Ibid., p. 25.

23 Day, *Union Square*, p. 21.

24 Day, *Long Loneliness*, p. 38.

25 Quoted in Robert Coles, *Dorothy Day: A Radical Devotion* (Boston: Da Capo Press, 1987), p. 138.

26 Day, *Union Square*, p. 10.

27 Day, *Long Loneliness*, p. 4.

28 Ibid., p. 44.

29 Miller, *Dorothy Day*, p. 56.

30 Day, *Long Loneliness*, p. 73.

31 See Miller, *Dorothy Day*, p. 100.

32 Forest, *Dorothy Day*, p. 43.

33 Day, *Long Loneliness*, p. 78.

34 Quoted in Forest, *Dorothy Day*, p. 271.

35 See Forest, *Dorothy Day*, pp. 271, 272.

36 Ibid., pp. 164, 165.

37 See Paul Elie, *The Life You Save May Be Your Own: An American Pilgrimage* (New York: Farrar, Straus and Giroux, 2003), p. 212.

[38] Hennessy, *Dorothy Day*, p. 184.

[39] Quoted in Day, *Selected Writings*, p. xxxix.

[40] See Forest, *Dorothy Day*, p. 284.

[41] Coles, *Dorothy Day*, pp. 62, 23.

[42] See Dorothy Day, *The Long Loneliness: The Autobiography of Dorothy Day* (New York: HarperSanFrancisco, 1952), p. 11.

[43] Ibid., p. 29.

[44] Dorothy Day, *From Union Square to Rome* (Maryknoll, New York: Orbis Books, 2006), p. 26.

[45] Ibid. p. 26.

[46] Quoted in Paul Elie, *The Life You Save May Be Your Own, An American Pilgrimage* (New York: Farrar, Straus and Giroux, 2003), 16.

[47] Day, *Union Square*, pp. 40, 42.

[48] Day, *Long Loneliness*, p. 45.

[49] Day, *Union Square*, p. 40.

[50] Ibid., p. 50.

[51] See Elie, *Life You Save*, p. 16.

[52] Day, *Union Square,* p. 53.

[53] Quoted in William D. Miller, *Dorothy Day: A Biography* (San Francisco: Harper & Row, 1982), p. 44.

[54] Ibid., p. 42.

[55] Quoted in Miller, *Dorothy Day*, p. 43.

[56] Day, *Union Square*, p. 55.

[57] Day, *Long Loneliness*, pp. 47, 48.

[58] Miller, *Dorothy Day*, p. 49.

[59] Ibid., p. 48.

[60] Quoted in Miller, *Dorothy Day*, p. 50.

[61] Quoted in Miller, *Dorothy Day*, p. 51.

[62] Quoted in Miller, *Dorothy Day*, p. 52.

[63] Day, *Long Loneliness*, p. 70.

64 Day, *Union Square*, p. 60.

65 Ibid., p. 55.

66 Ibid., pp. 62, 63.

67 Dorothy Day, The *Long Loneliness: The Autobiography of Dorothy Day* (New York: HarperSanFrancisco, 1952), p. 66.

68 Paul Elie, *The Life You Save May be Your Own: An American Pilgrimage* (New York: Farrar, Straus and Giroux, 2003), p. 27.

69 Dorothy Day, *From Union Square to Rome* (Maryknoll, New York: Orbis Books, 2006), pp. 89, 90.

70 Quoted in William D. Miller, D*orothy Day: A Biography* (San Francisco: Harper & Row, 1982), p. 59.

71 Dorothy Day, *Selected Writings: By Little and By Little*, ed. Robert Ellsberg (Maryknoll, New York: Orbis Books, 1992), p. 149.

72 Quoted in Miller, *Dorothy Day*, p. 71.

73 Quoted in Miller, *Dorothy Day*, p. 71.

74 Quoted in Miller, *Dorothy Day*, p. 69.

75 Quoted in Miller, *Dorothy Day*, p. 68.

76 Quoted in Jim Forest, *All Is Grace: A Biography Dorothy Day* (Maryknoll, New York: Orbis Books, 2011), p. 35.

77 Kate Hennessy, *Dorothy Day: The World Will Be Saved by Beauty: An Intimate Portrait of My Grandmother* (New York: Scribner, 2017), p. 4.

78 See Miller, *Dorothy Day*, p. 95.

79 See Hennessy, *Dorothy Day*, 13.

80 Elie, *Life You Save*, p. 27.

81 Hennessy, *Dorothy Day*, p. 17.

82 Quoted in Miller, *Dorothy Day,* p. 109.

83 Quoted in Miller, *Dorothy Day*, p. 108.

84 Hennessy, *Dorothy Day*, p. 16.

85 Day, *Union Square*, p. 90.

86 Hennessy, *Dorothy Day*, p. 8.

87 Miller, *Dorothy Day*, p. 107.

88 Hennessy, *Dorothy Day*, p. 15.

89 Quoted in Miller, *Dorothy Day*, p. 110.

90 Miller, *Dorothy Day*, p. 107.

91 Day, *Long Loneliness*, p. 84.

92 Day, *Union Square*, p. 90.

93 Elie, *Life You Save*, p. 28.

94 Day, *Union Square*, p. 91.

95 See Forest, *Dorothy Day*, p. 31.

96 Quoted in Forest, *Dorothy Day*, p. 47.

97 Quoted in Miller, *Dorothy Day*, pp. 117, 118.

98 Vatican ll, Pastoral Constitution on the Church in the Modern World, paragraph 18, ed. Austin Flannery, O.P. (Collegeville: Liturgical Press, 1975).

99 Dorothy Day, *The Long Loneliness:, The Autobiography of Dorothy Day* (New York: HarperSanFrancisco, 1952), p. 88.

100 Quoted in William D. Miller, *Dorothy Day: A Biography* (San Francisco: Harper & Row, 1982), p. 119.

101 Day, *Long Loneliness*, pp. 90, 91.

102 Ibid., p. 91.

103 Quoted in Miller, *Dorothy Day*, p. 124.

104 See Miller, *Dorothy Day,* 125.

105 Kate Hennessy, *Dorothy Day: The World Will Be Saved by Beauty: An Intimate Portrait of my Grandmother* (New York: Scribner, 2017), p. 24.

106 Quoted in Miller, *Dorothy Day*, p. 125.

107 Quoted in Miller, *Dorothy Day*, p. 128.

108 Hennessy, *Dorothy Day*, p. 24.

109 See Jim Forest*, All Is Grace: A Biography of Dorothy Day* (Maryknoll, New York: Orbis Books, 2011), pp. 51, 52.

[110] Quoted in Miller, *Dorothy Day*, pp. 126, 127.

[111] Hennessy, *Dorothy Day*, p. 25.

[112] Forest, *Dorothy Day*, p. 52.

[113] Quoted in Miller, *Dorothy Day*, pp. 129, 130.

[114] Quoted in Miller, *Dorothy Day*, p. 130.

[115] Quoted in Miller, *Dorothy Day*, pp. 131, 132.

[116] Quoted in Miller, *Dorothy Day*, p. 132.

[117] Quoted in Forest, *Dorothy Day*, p. 54.

[118] See Hennessy, *Dorothy Day*, pp. 28, 29.

[119] See Forest, *Dorothy Day*, p. 54.

[120] See Laura Michele Diener, 'The Habit of Being Passionate: Dorothy Day's Radical Mysticism', *Numero Cinq* 7(5), August 2016, http://numerocinqmagazine.com/2016/08/03/78027/.

[121] See Forest, *Dorothy Day*, p. 55.

[122] Quoted in Forest, *Dorothy Day*, p. 57.

[123] Hennessy, *Dorothy Day*, p. 30.

[124] Quoted in Miller, *Dorothy Day*, p., 143.

[125] Hennessy, *Dorothy Day*, p. 33.

[126] Ibid., p. 33.

[127] Day, *Long Loneliness*, p. 104.

[128] Ibid., p. 106.

[129] Quoted in Forest, *Dorothy Day,* 62.

[130] William D. Miller, *Dorothy Day: A Biography* (San Francisco: Harper & Row, 1982), pp. 165, 166.

[131] Ibid., p. 170.

[132] Dorothy Day, *From Union Square to Rome* (Maryknoll, New York: Orbis Books, 2006), p. 117.

[133] Ibid., p. 117.

[134] Dorothy Day, *The Long Loneliness:, The Autobiography of Dorothy Day* (New York: HarperSanFrancisco), 1952), p. 116.

[135] Day, *Union Square*, p. 122.

[136] Day, *Long Loneliness*, p. 116.

[137] Kate Hennessy, *Dorothy Day: The World Will Be Saved by Beauty: An Intimate Portrait of My Grandmother* (New York: Scribner, 2017), p. 43.

[138] Dorothy Day, *All the Way to Heaven: The Selected Letters of Dorothy Day*, ed. Robert Ellsberg (New York: Image Books, 2010), p. 11.

[139] Day, *Way to Heaven*, p. 15.

[140] Miller, *Dorothy Day*, p. 168.

[141] Day, *Long Loneliness*, p. 120.

[142] Miller, *Dorothy Day*, p. 168.

[143] Day, *Long Loneliness*, pp. 118, 119.

[144] Ibid., p. 135.

[145] Day, *Way to Heaven*, p. 17.

[146] Day, *Long Loneliness*, pp. 135, 136.

[147] Ibid., p. 132.

[148] Ibid., pp. 132, 133.

[149] Ibid., p. 134.

[150] Ibid., p. 136.

[151] Ibid., p. 137.

[152] Ibid., p. 141.

[153] Ibid., p. 142.

[154] Ibid., pp. 142, 143.

[155] Ibid., p. 143.

[156] Ibid., pp. 143, 144.

[157] Ibid., p. 148.

[158] Ibid., p. 140.

[159] Ibid., pp. 148, 149.

[160] Day, *Union Square,* p. 146.

[161] See Day, *Way to Heaven,* p. 61.

162 Quoted in Miller, *Dorothy Day*, p. 212.

163 Day*, Way to Heaven*, pp. 29, 30.

164 Ibid., pp. 34, 36.

165 Ibid., pp. 61, 62.

166 Ibid., pp. 63.

167 Ibid., p. 216

168 Day, *Long Loneliness*, p. 140.

169 Quoted in Jim Forest, *All Is Grace: A Biography of Dorothy Day* (Maryknoll, New York: Orbis Books, 2011), pp. 2, 3.

170 See Forest, *Dorothy Day*, p. 98.

171 Dorothy Day, *The Long Loneliness: The Autobiography of Dorothy Day* (New York: HarperSanFrancisco, 1952), p. 165.

172 Ibid., p. 165.

173 Robert Coles, *Dorothy Day: A Radical Devotion (*Boston: Da Capo Press, 1987), p. 11.

174 Day, *Long Loneliness,* p. 166.

175 Ibid., p. 169.

176 Ibid., p. 169.

177 Quoted in Forest, *Dorothy Day*, p. 105.

178 Peter Maurin, *The Forgotten Radical*, ed. Lincoln Rice (New York: Fordham University Press, 2020), p. 105.

179 Ibid., p. 76.

180 See William D. Miller, *Dorothy Day, A Biography* (San Francisco: Harper & Row, 1982), p. 251.

181 Quoted in Miller, *Dorothy Day*, p. 228.

182 Quoted in Forest, *Dorothy Day*, p. 107.

183 Dorothy Day, *House of Hospitality* (Huntington: Our Sunday Visitor Publishing Division, 2015), pp. 40, 41.

184 Quoted in Kate Hennessy, *Dorothy Day: The World Will Be Saved by Beauty: An Intimate Portrait of My Grandmother* (New York: Scribner, 2017), p. 73.

185 Day, *House of Hospitality*, p. 41.

186 Ibid., p. 44.

187 Hennessy*, Dorothy Day*, p. 87.

188 Quoted in Forest, *Dorothy Day*, p. 130.

189 Dorothy Day, *Loaves and Fishes: The Inspiring Story of the Catholic Worker Movement* (Maryknoll, New York: Orbis Books, 1963), p. 91.

190 See Maurin, *Forgotten Radical*, p. 363.

191 Ibid., p. 364.

192 Hennessy, *Dorothy Day*, p. 153.

193 Day, *Long Loneliness*, p. 278.

194 Ibid., p. 279.

195 Quoted in Forest, *Dorothy Day*, p. 186.

196 Dorothy Day, *All the Way to Heaven: The Selected Letters of Dorothy Day,* ed. Robert Ellsberg (New York: Image Books, 2010), pp. 290, 291.

197 See Maurin, *Forgotten Radical*, p. 14.

198 https://www.catholicworker.org

199 Quoted in William D. Miller, *Dorothy Day: A Biography* (San Francisco: Harper & Row, 1982), p. 404.

200 Dorothy Day, *All the Way to Heaven: The Selected Letters of Dorothy Day,* ed. Robert Ellsberg (New York: Image Books, 2010), pp. 218, 219, 220.

201 Day, W*ay to Heaven*, pp. 245, 246, 247.

202 Dorothy Day, *Selected Writings: By Little and By Little,* ed. Robert Ellsberg (Maryknoll, New York: Orbis Books, 1992), p. 169.

203 Day, *Selected Writings*, p. 172.

204 Quoted in Robert Coles, *Dorothy Day: A Radical Devotion* (Boston: Da Capo Press, 1987), pp. 82, 83.

205 Day, *Selected Writings*, p. 334.

206 Coles, *Dorothy Day*, p. 67.

207 Dorothy Day, *The Long Loneliness: The Autobiography of Dorothy* Day (New York: HarperSanFrancisco, 1952), p. 218.

208 Day, *Long Loneliness*, p. 149.

209 Quoted in Coles, *Dorothy Day*, pp. 76, 77.

210 Dorothy Day, *From Union Square to Rome* (Maryknoll, New York: Orbis Books, 2006), p. 137.

211 Day, *Long Loneliness*, p. 150.

212 Quoted in Coles, *Dorothy Day*, p. 82.

213 See Ignazio Silone, *Bread and Wine* (New York: Signet Classics, 1986), p. 184.

214 Coles, *Dorothy Day*, pp. 149, 170.

215 Irving Howe, Introduction to *Bread and Wine,* V.

216 Silone, *Bread and Wine*, pp. 168, 171.

217 Howe, Introduction to *Bread and Wine,* VII.

218 Day, *Long Loneliness*, p. 79.

219 See Day, *Union Square*, p. 177.

220 Day, *Long Loneliness*, pp. 165, 166.

221 Quoted in Paul Elie, *The Life You Save May Be Your Own: An American Pilgrimage* (New York: Farrar, Straus and Giroux, 2003), p. 245.

222 Dorothy Day, *Selected Writings: By Little and By Little*, ed. Robert Ellsberg (Maryknoll, New York: Orbis Books, 1992), p. xviii.

223 Quoted in Jim Forest, *All Is Grace: A Biography of Dorothy Day* (Maryknoll, New York: Orbis Books, 2011), p. 180.

224 Quoted in William D. Miller, *All is Grace: The Spirituality of Dorothy Day* (New York: Doubleday & Company, 1987), p. 106.

[225] Dorothy Day, *The Long Loneliness: The Autobiography of Dorothy Day* (New York: HarperSanFrancisco, 1952), p. 263.

[226] Quoted in Kate Hennessy, *Dorothy Day: The World Will Be Saved by Beauty: An Intimate Portrait of my Grandmother* (New York: Scribner, 2017), p. 259.

[227] Robert Coles, *Dorothy Day: A Radical Devotion* (Boston: Da Capo Press, 1987), pp. 119, 97.

[228] Ibid., pp. 102, 101.

[229] Dorothy Day, *From Union Square to Rome* (Maryknoll, New York: Orbis Books, 2006), p. 155.

[230] Dorothy Day, *The Duty of Delight: The Diaries of Dorothy Day*, ed. Robert Ellsberg (New York: Image Books, 2011), p. 100.

[231] Quoted in Mark and Louise Zwick, *The Catholic Worker Movement: Intellectual and Spiritual Origins* (Mahwah, New Jersey: Paulist Press, 2005), p. 240.

[232] Quoted in Forest, *Dorothy Day*, p. 177.

[233] Quoted in Hennessy, *Dorothy Day*, p. 130.

[234] Quoted in Miller, *Spirituality*, p. 48.

[235] Miller, *Spirituality*, p. 1.

[236] Ibid., p. 2.

[237] Ibid., p. 3.

[238] Coles, *Dorothy Day*, p. 94.

[239] Zwick and Zwick, *Catholic Worker,* 247.

[240] Ibid, p. 247.

[241] Ibid, p. 248.

[242] Coles, *Dorothy Day*, p. 143.

[243] Dorothy Day, *On Pilgrimage* (Grand Rapids: William B. Eerdmans Publishing Company, 1999), pp. viii, ix.

[244] Quoted in Forest, *Dorothy Day*, p. 325.

[245] See Forest, *Dorothy Day*, p. 325.

246 Quoted in Coles, *Dorothy Day*, pp. 126, 116, 95, 122.

247 Coles, *Dorothy Day*, p. 115.

248 Quoted in Paul Elie, *The Life You Save May Be Your Own: An American Pilgrimage* (New York: Farrar, Straus and Giroux, 2003), p. 446.

249 Dorothy Day, *The Long Loneliness: The Autobiography of Dorothy Day* (New York: HarperSanFrancisco, 1952), p. 20.

250 Dorothy Day, *From Union Square to Rome* (Maryknoll, New York: Orbis Books, 2006), p. 123.

251 Ibid., p. 148.

252 William D. Miller, *All is Grace: The Spirituality of Dorothy Day* (New York: Doubleday & Company, 1987), p. 195.

253 Dorothy Day, *Selected Writing, By Little and By Little,* Ed. Robert Ellsberg (Maryknoll, New York: Orbis Books, 1992), xxxviii.

254 Coles, *Dorothy Day,* 16.

255 See Forest, *Dorothy Day,* 302.

Select Bibliography

Brooks, David. *The Road to Character.* New York: Random House, 2015.

Coles, Robert. *Dorothy Day: A Radical Devotion.* Boston: Da Capo Press, 1987.

Day, Dorothy. *All the Way to Heaven, The Selected Letters of Dorothy Day.* Ed. Robert Ellsberg. New York: Image Books, 2010.

Day, Dorothy. *The Duty of Delight: The Diaries of Dorothy Day.* Ed. Robert Ellsberg. New York: Image Books, 2008.

Day, Dorothy. *The Eleventh Virgin.* New York: A. and C. Boni, 1924.

Day, Dorothy. *From Union Square to Rome,* 2nd edn. Maryknoll New York: Orbis Books, 2006 (first published 1938).

Day, Dorothy. *House of Hospitality.* Huntington: Our Sunday Visitor Publishing Division, 2015.

Day, Dorothy. *Loaves and Fishes: The Inspiring Story of the Catholic Worker Movement.* Maryknoll, New York: Orbis Books, 1997.

Day, Dorothy. *The Long Loneliness: The Autobiography of Dorothy Day.* New York: HarperSanFrancisco, 1952.

Day, Dorothy. *Meditations.* Selected and arranged by Stanley Vishnewski. New York: Newman Press, 1970.

Day, Dorothy. *On Pilgrimage.* Grand Rapids: William B. Eerdmans Publishing Company, 1999.

Day, Dorothy. *Selected Writings: By Little and By Little,* ed. Robert Ellsberg. Maryknoll, New York: Orbis Books, 1992.

Day, Dorothy. *Thérèse.* Notre Dame, Indiana: Christian Classics, 2016.

Diener, Laura Michele. 'The Habit of Being Passionate: Dorothy Day's Radical Mysticism', *Numero Cinq* 7(5), http://numerocinqmagazine.com/2016/08/03/78027.

Elie, Paul. *The Life You Save May Be Your Own: An American Pilgrimage.* New York: Farrar, Straus and Giroux, 2003.

Forest, Jim. *All Is Grace: A Biography of Dorothy Day.* Maryknoll, New York: Orbis Books, 2011.

Hennessy, Kate. *Dorothy Day: The World Will Be Saved by Beauty: An Intimate Portrait of My Grandmother.* New York: Scribner, 2017.

Howe, Irving. 'Introduction', Ignazio Silone, *Bread and Wine.* New York: Signet Classics, 1986.

Maurin, Peter. *The Forgotten Radical,* ed. Lincoln Rice. New York: Fordham University Press, 2020.

Miller, William D. *Dorothy Day: A Biography.* San Francisco: Harper & Row, 1982.

Miller, William D. *All is Grace: The Spirituality of Dorothy Day.* New York: Doubleday & Company, 1987.

Silone, Ignazio. *Bread and Wine.* New York: Signet Classics, 1986.

Zwick, Mark and Louise. *The Catholic Worker Movement: Intellectual and Spiritual Origins.* New York: Paulist Press, 2005.